DINEDOR & ROTHERWAS
EXPLORED

Opposite: 'Hereford and River Wye from Dinedor Hill', an engraving from a painting by David Cox which was one of the illustrations in Thomas Roscoe's Wanderings and Excursions in South Wales including the Scenery of the River Wye.

DINEDOR & ROTHERWAS EXPLORED

by

Dinedor Heritage Group

Logaston Press

LOGASTON PRESS
Little Logaston Woonton Almeley
Herefordshire HR3 6QH
logastonpress.co.uk

First published by Logaston Press 2014
Copyright © of each chapter is vested in its author 2014

ISBN 978 1 906663 88 9

Typeset by Logaston Press
and printed and bound in Poland by
www.lfbookservices.co.uk

Cover photograph courtesy of Haydn Lloyd

Contents

Dinidor Hill

Behold yon Hill's aspiring brow
Resplendent shines on all below
She's clad in Summer's green array
Bedeck'd with flowerets fresh and gay.
The Wye's meand'ring stream doth glide
And moistens well her verdant side:
The birds they chant their choral lay
And lovers there still wend their way;
And whisper talks of ardent love,
And kisses press their love to prove;
Seated by the Wye's bright rill,
They bless the shades of Dinidor Hill.

They talk of hills and vales in Wales
Rich mountains girt by flowing dales:
The Alp's hoar brow of Italy's boast,
But this shall be my constant toast.
The Hill on which the clouds ne'er rest
But the sun's bright rays illume his breast
Let them boast who rove far and near,
And seek fresh joys from shore to shore,
But I shall ne'er delight to roam,
But sip my pleasures here at home
Encircled by the Wye's bright rill
I still shall bless the shades of Dinidor Hill.

My home! my home! my native home,
It sounds as charms wherein I roam,
I look with joy on this loved sod
Whereof my infant feet have trod,
The cot wherein I first drew breath!
The cot wherein I'll welcome death.
The Castle Green – the Bassam mead,
The school where germed by learned seed.
Nor will I blush to own that they,
Were sown by warm heart charity
And grateful will I be until
The sun shall cease to shine on Dinidor Hill.

Thomas Vaughan, 1836

Acknowledgements

Dinedor Heritage Group wishes to acknowledge the extensive range of advice, information and encouragement that it has received in the production of this publication. Without this help the project would never have got off the ground.

This publication is not, nor was ever intended to be, some great literary masterpiece; nevertheless we trust that you will find the contents informative and interesting. No two people remember events in an identical manner and so contradictions and errors may well occur. Each contributor has brought to the publication their own unique and individual style.

Those that have submitted chapters are acknowledged at the outset of their work but there are also many others that have contributed behind the scenes, these include: Margaret Brown, Eileen Buckle, Andrew Clifton, John (Harry) Davies, Valerie Done, Bryan and Ann Edwards, Barbara Ferris, Tracey Goodwin, Robert Gorman, Mary Grice, Alison Hall, Liz and Jane Hicks, David Hill, Melvyn Holmes, Derrick Jones, Jimmy Joynt, Alexandra Kitchener, Rosemary Lillico, David Lovelace, Ros Morris, Jean Owen, Mike Patrick, Jean Payne, David Price, Jean Savage, Reg South and David Whitehead. In addition we would like to thank, Dinedor P.C.C., The Derek Foxton Archives, Hereford Library, Hereford Records Office, Herefordshire Lore, St Martins Church Office and Hereford Cathedral Library for their help, support and, in some cases, use of illustrations.

The Group would also like to thank the following for giving permission to quote from their works: Heather Hurley, *The Hereford Times*, The Woolhope Naturalists' Field Club, Myrtle Middleton and Jenny Smith.

We also owe a debt of gratitude to Chris Over for co-ordinating the efforts of the authors of the chapters and to Andy and Karen Johnson of Logaston Press for their editorial guidance and expertise in the production of this book; most of us, after all, are just a group of enthusiastic, amateur historians with a love for our surroundings and its rich history. Also to Border Office Supplies & Systems Ltd for the never ending provision of photo-copying facilities.

And, finally, all of this would not have been possible without the initial generosity of The Heritage Lottery Fund.

Dinedor Heritage Group will continue to build up an archive of all things connected with Dinedor, Rotherwas and surrounding areas and would appreciate any contributions that help to achieve this.

Do visit our website dinedorheritagegroup.wordpress.com.

Lines written on Dinedor Hill

Sweet spot of song! I seek thy breast
To muse awhile, unchecked and free;
As wearied birds that seek a nest,
And shelter neath the spreading tree,
I come to lose the sense of ill,
Amid thy shades, sweet Dinedor Hill.

Far from life's crowd and clamour rude,
With wearied frame and fevered brow;
My spirit courts thy solitude,
Since the gay throng forsakes thee now,
And all around is hushed and still,
Save my lone step on Dinedor Hill.

Joy haunted spot! remembrance turns
Far from this scene of peace and thee,
The bounds of time fond fancy spurns,
And brings me back to childhood's glee
And hours when I have ranged at will
In boyhood's bloom on Dinedor Hill.

Sweet spot of song; when I am gone,
Some loftier Bard may wake thy praise:
Haply while musing thus alone,
He flies the 'hum of men', to gaze
On Nature; spoil her how they will,
She'll still be Queen on Dinedor Hill.

This poem, ascribed simply to 'John',
appeared in the *Hereford Journal* in July 1835

Preface

This book came about because a group of people got together in 2007 to learn more about their village. It is part of a continuing story and reflects how sharing experiences develops community spirit. As we shared our interests and raised more questions, we were humbled by the response and realised our findings deserved wider appreciation. We trust this book goes some way towards fulfilling that aim, and will give those who live in or are otherwise somehow attached to the area a greater understanding of the community and its past, and a deeper association with its landscape.

We are indebted to the expertise and passion of people who have inspired Dinedor Heritage Group in talks and guided tours. The former have included: 'The Dinedor Secret Army' by David Seeney; 'Local Stories' by Bill Laws; 'Heritage beyond Rotherwas' by Ian Bapty; 'Exploring Dinedor's Past' by Dr Sylvia Pinches & Chris Atkinson; 'Rotherwas – Living Legacy' by Hugh Heatherwick; 'Exploring Dinedor Hill' by Phil Rickman & Chris Hinsley; 'Dinedor, Past & Present' by Heather Hurley; 'Developing the Rotherwas Site' by Andrew Leitch; 'Rotherwas Women' by Julie Orton-Davies and 'Rotherwas Heritage & Access Links by Mairead Lane, Mark Edwards & Mark Pierce. In addition, and linking our area with wider Herefordshire, there have been talks on Alfred Watkins, strategy and policy regarding archaeological finds, Iron Age to medieval pottery, the Dorstone dig, evenings where people have shared memories and open days where exhibitions have been mounted. Guided tours have included ones to the site of Rotherwas House Site with Chris Over & Nicola Goodwin, and to Hill Farm, Castle Frome, with its restored medieval fishponds.

We were intrigued by one particular site in the parish, where lumps and bumps possibly indicated a deserted medieval village. We determined to establish what lay beneath the surface and persevered through three attempts before winning approval from English Heritage and gaining Lottery funding in 2012. What we discovered from the resulting digs is all included here, together with digests of Rotherwas explorations to date – all made available by Herefordshire Archaeology for us to publicise. We have brought together the work of many people – professional and amateur. Some have delved into the archives and old directories to unearth information, others have had an interest in a particular aspect of local life over many years, and many have shared their memories or set down some history of the farm or house in which they live or have lived.

This book is the culmination of our initial project but just the beginning of our interest. We expect to work closely with our Parish Council, the Enterprise Zone, Herefordshire Council and other local history groups to care for our heritage centres and coordinate footpath and information boards. We look forward to many more talks, tours and exhibitions in the coming years. Whatever your reason for picking up this book, we hope you will make a personal connection with what you read and look at the area with fresh eyes. Perhaps it will encourage you to visit it if, until now, it has been comparatively unknown to you. Others will hopefully be stirred to contribute to our story – in person or on our website. There is so much more to discover.

Barbara Ferris
Chairman
Dinedor Heritage Group
dinedorheritagegroup.wordpress.com

Dinedor

Dinedor! in childhood's careless hour
I joy'd thy brow to gain,
In triumph snatch'd a token flower,
To prove my toil not vain;
But soon with other eyes I went,
O'er traces of past ages bent,
On nature's treasures gaz'd intent,
Till from thy haunts my ripen'd fancy drew
Treasures exhaustless yet, and interest ever new.

Sweet crested upland! beauteous knoll!
Lov'd in life's early stage,
So, as the dark years downward roll,
The solace of my age;
Still let me find some unknown nook,
Still by thy side read nature's book,
Still on the varied landscape look
The leafy ringlets round thy summit curl'd,
And spreading at thy feet the garden of the world.

This poem appeared, unattributed,
in the *Hereford Journal* in June 1837

1 Dinedor; an Introduction

by Chris Atkinson, B.A., M.A.

The ancient parish of Dinedor is situated within the County of Herefordshire under 2.5km from the centre of the City of Hereford and located on the opposite bank of the River Wye to the north-west. It is the Wye that delineates the northern and eastern extent of the parish as it gently meanders south towards Ross-on-Wye and Monmouth.

To the south the parish boundary follows the original sinuous course of the Tar's Brook, which today takes on a far more linear course after it was rerouted for the purpose of

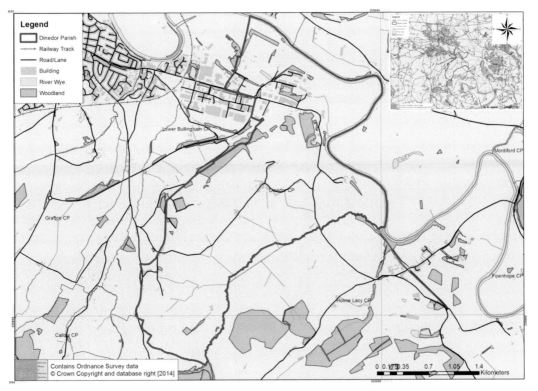

Map showing the location and extent of Dinedor Parish

supplying Dinedor Mill. Dinedor parish's western boundary runs south through Rotherwas Enterprise Zone, beyond which it traverses the north-facing slope of Dinedor Hill before following the north/south orientated lane that links the summit of Dinedor Hill with the hamlet of Dinedor Cross.

In all, the land enclosed by these boundaries today measures 1,667.72 acres (674.905 hectares). Arguably still the most dominant feature of the area today just as throughout its history is that of Dinedor Hill (182m above sea level); a prominent south-west to north-east aligned ridgeline of interbedded argillaceous rocks and sandstone of the St Maughan's Formation which in essence divides the fertile alluvial plains attributed to the Tar's Brook in the south from the river terrace deposits attributed to the River Wye in the north and east. Underlying the alluvial and river terrace deposits, the solid geology consists primarily of interbedded siltstones and mudstones of the Raglan Mudstone Formation of the Silurian era.[1]

Nestled into the foot of the south-facing slope of the Dinedor ridgeline is the village core of Dinedor itself, straddling a narrow lane that traverses the south face of the ridgeline linking the Holme Lacy Road to the east with the main route to Hoarwithy to the west. At the centre of the village, set away from the modern road to the south, is the parish church of St Andrew's (the county's Historic Environment Record [HER] number 1279), a structure which, although largely rebuilt during the 19th century, can trace its origins to at least as far back as the 13th century.

Elsewhere, settlement is centred upon the slopes at the western end of the Dinedor ridge whose summit is dominated by the ancient hill top enclosure of Dinedor Camp, as well as at the foot of the ridge to the east where scattered settlement is located around the vicinity of Dinedor Court. A fourth area of settlement is located within the north of the parish at Rotherwas, the location of what was once the seat of the Bodenham family.

A number of what might be regarded as myths and legends have arisen concerning sites across the parish of Dinedor. One of the most famous is the reference to Bloody Meadow, a field name recorded on the 1840 Tithe Map and located within the south of the parish adjacent to the Tar's Brook, where excavation as part of drainage works in the 19th century uncovered a pit full of horse bones (HER 33637). As a result the site has been attributed to a battle that took place in 1055 when the deposed Saxon earl Ælfgar led an army of Irish and Welsh against England. Prior to reaching Hereford his army was met by an English mounted force led by Earl Ralph. However, as the Abingdon Chronicle of the Anglo Saxon Chronicles reads

> … before a spear was thrown, the English fled, because they had been made to fight on horseback. Many of them were slain, about four hundred or perhaps five, but none of their opponents, who went to the town (Hereford) and burned it to the ground.[2]

One of the earliest written accounts of Dinedor Camp (also known as Oyster Camp) comes from the *Imperial Gazetteer of England and Wales* compiled by John Marius Wilson and published in 1872: '… Dinedor Hill is crowned by a Roman camp, supposed to be that of Ostorius Scapula; and commands a lovely view'.[3]

Publius Ostorius Scapula was the governor of Britain between 47 and 52AD. It was during this period that the British warlord/freedom fighter Caratacus was finally defeated in

View from Dinedor Hill looking towards Hereford around 1810

battle by the Romans somewhere in what is today mid Wales, which at the time was within the tribal territory of the Ordovices.[4] In an act of consolidation, Scapula commanded the establishment of a defensive frontier – which was thought to include Dinedor Hill – against the tribal territories to the west. However, to date, while archaeological investigations at Dinedor Camp have uncovered evidence for both Bronze Age and Iron Age settlement, very little evidence has been found to suggest Roman activity.

Beyond references to historical events, a rapid assessment online of the county's Historic Environment Record provides us with an at-a-glance a list of 62 individual sites within the parish (not including finds of single items) relating to the activities of humans over time. Although the list is limited – in its absence of sites yet to be uploaded onto the database, as well as the need for security in regards to providing exact site grid references in certain circumstances – it does enlighten the casual researcher to just how much of a rich heritage there is within a relatively small parish. Human activity can be traced within the parish to as early as the Mesolithic (9,600-4,000BC) and continued through the Neolithic (4,000-2,500BC), Bronze Age (2,500-750BC) and Iron Age (750BC-43AD). With the exception of individual find spots along the summit of the Dinedor ridgeline and the Bronze/Iron Age hilltop enclosure of Dinedor Camp, most discoveries have been due to archaeological investigations in advance of modern development centred within what is now the Rotherwas Enterprise Zone located in the north of the parish. As a result of this research and excavations our understanding of patterns of prehistoric settlement and ritual landscapes has substantially increased.

Beyond the evidence for prehistory, Roman activity in the form of rural farmsteads and land divisions has also been identified across the north of the parish. It is during the medieval period, however, that one of the earliest written records mentions settlement throughout the parish with centres based around the manor of Rotherwas and Dinedor village. The most substantial impact upon the parish came in the post-medieval and modern periods with significant alterations made to land division and use, increased settlement and, following the onset of the First World War, the establishment of the National Filling Factory at Rotherwas in 1916.

It is this rich and varied history that enthused the community of Dinedor and led to their establishment of the Dinedor Heritage Group with the aim of exploring their local heritage and promoting it to the public. Following a successful application to the Heritage Lottery Fund's Your Heritage Scheme in 2012, the Dinedor Origins Project obtained funding and commenced with the goal of disseminating the results of both past and recent archaeological/ historical discoveries.

In support of the documentary research, the Dinedor Heritage Group carried out a series of community based archaeological investigations centred on the enhancement of the parish's medieval heritage. The investigations actively involved members of the public from across the county and beyond as well as students of Hereford Sixth Form College and local schools.

2   The Prehistory of Dinedor & Rotherwas

by Ian Stead & Tim Hoverd

The origins of human settlement in and around Dinedor are shrouded in mystery. Archaeological investigations over the last decade have provided tantalising glimpses into this past, suggesting a complex and intensive series of relationships between this landscape and its people. The topography of Dinedor and the surrounding area is varied, encompassing Dinedor Hill, rising to a height of 182 metres above sea level, gently undulating terrain and part of the Wye Valley flood plain.

The area lies approximately six miles to the south of the southernmost extent of the ice sheets of the last glaciation (112,000 to 12,000 years ago), meaning that the area would have been accessible to seasonal hunter gatherers during the Palaeolithic period. The discovery of a Palaeolithic stone axe in Tupsley in 1977 is testament to their presence within the close environs. Three other axes of this date have been found in the county. Small quantities of 'microliths' (small flint blades and other tools) have been recovered from a number of sites in and around Hereford indicating the presence of Mesolithic (6000-4000BC) habitation in the area.

Pollen records from sites in the county suggest that as the temperature rose between 10000BC and 6000BC the tundra grassland gave way to broadleaf forest. These same records illustrate the sudden and rapid decline of tree cover during the fourth millennium BC corresponding to an equally sudden and rapid rise in grasses and cereals suggesting that this marks the first major impact of humankind upon the region. The Neolithic period (4000-2800BC) is generally accepted as being the beginnings of a permanently settled farming system rather than the subsistence hunter gathering which occurred during the Mesolithic (8000-4000BC). The chance finds of Neolithic flints and fragments of polished axes within Dinedor and in neighbouring parishes, suggests that by the fourth millennium BC Dinedor, along with much, if not all, of what is now Herefordshire, had been settled by a people who were not only skilled farmers but also belonged to a society which had complex beliefs, hierarchies and ties not only to similar communities within the rest of Britain but in continental Europe as well.

The Rotherwas Ribbon

The ritual and symbolism apparently so important in Neolithic society has been well documented in many parts of Britain. Neolithic funerary monuments in the form of long barrows, cursus and causewayed enclosures are well known in most counties. In Herefordshire, however, until recently evidence for such sites was meagre with only a handful of monuments known to be of Neolithic date being recorded. Fieldwork over the last 15 years has begun to rectify this situation. Increased aerial survey, nationally funded research projects and development-led archaeological investigations, have led not only to the discovery of Neolithic sites similar to those found in other counties, but

Two views of the excavation of the Rotherwas Ribbon, showing the undulating nature of the 'path', the stones used in the surface and some of the excavation pits and trenches.

types of site which appear to be unique to this region. Such sites are, by their very nature and age, enigmatic, often leaving everyone (including professional archaeologists) unclear as to their exact purpose and use.

One such site was discovered during archaeological excavations undertaken in advance of the construction of part of the Rotherwas Access Road during 2007. This comprised a sinuous strip of gravel, quartz and burnt stone laid as a surface within a shallow depression. It appears to run from the lower slopes of Dinedor Hill towards the River Wye and its flood plain. It is believed that the burnt stones were purposely used in the construction of two surfaces, one below the other, indicating that the monument was used during two separate phases. The burnt, or fire cracked, stones are thought to have been used as pot boilers (stones heated in a fire and when red hot put into pots in order to boil water or heat food), for Neolithic pottery could not withstand being hung directly over a fire. Analysis of the soils associated with this unique feature suggest that its builders used a dried up stream channel as a base for its construction and, where necessary, modified the natural topography in order to create a feature which not only meandered from side to side, and varied in width from 5 metres to 8 metres, but which also used parts of the channel sides in order to appear more three dimensional. Evaluation excavations suggest that this feature is over 350 metres in length. Its sinuous course quickly earned it the nickname of 'The Rotherwas Ribbon'. Finds associated with this remarkable feature, together with a series of carbon 14 dates suggest that the oldest surface was in use towards the end of the Neolithic period and that the later surface was used during the Bronze Age. Whatever this nationally important and fascinating feature was used for (a question which will occupy archaeologists' minds, both locally and nationally, for some time to come), it is clear that the communities which constructed and maintained it did so over a very long period of time (over half a millennia) and that it was therefore of great symbolic and or ritual importance to the population of Dinedor, Rotherwas and the surrounding area. The favoured suggestion to date is that the Ribbon was used in some form of processional event in which people walked its length and deposited small fragments of flint, animal bone and, occasionally, human bone. It is believed that as part of this ritual a series of pits was dug either side of the Ribbon into which artefacts were placed. As a result of the Ribbon's discovery, the part of the road which was to be constructed across it was re-designed so as to leave the Ribbon undamaged and protected beneath the new road.

Other Neolithic and Bronze Age finds
Further archaeological fieldwork was undertaken close to the Ribbon in advance of the infrastructure works for the south magazine area of the Rotherwas industrial estate. This work has produced evidence for the creation and use of an enclosure covering a massive area and defined by a small bank and ditch. Within the enclosed area were spreads of burnt stone associated with pits and troughs, possibly providing a source for the burned / fire cracked stone used in the construction of the Ribbon.

Archaeological survey within the fields between Green Crize, the Hoarwithy Road and the new relief road recovered evidence of farming and domestic activity suggesting that this area had been intensively farmed from at least the early Bronze Age. Flints and pottery were found alongside fragments of charred hazelnut shell and burnt clay which indicates the use of fires and domestic activity. On a natural high spot overlooking the Red Brook finds of carbonised oats and burnt bone are believed to date from the Middle Bronze Age, and there is also some evidence for the presence of a cremation burial. Analysis of the soils showed that colluvium was deposited there at some time between 2500-1100BC. For the colluvium to have formed (colluvium being soil washed from hill tops and slopes into valley bottoms and other low points) the surrounding area must have been cleared of trees and under permanent, long term cultivation. Neolithic flint tools and flakes have been found below Dinedor Ridge and recently at Hill Farm below the western slopes of Dinedor Camp. A Neolithic polished stone axe was found at Dinedor Camp and a Bronze Age flint arrowhead was also found in the field above Dinedor village below the ridge of Dinedor Hill. Evidence of further Neolithic occupation in the form of flints, polished axe fragments and pottery has been recovered from the slope north of Dinedor village.

It is clear from the archaeological fieldwork undertaken in and around Rotherwas and Dinedor that this part of Herefordshire was heavily populated from at least the Late Neolithic period and throughout the Bronze Age. The mixture of domestic and ritual or symbolic features, together with evidence of farming, suggests that these populations thrived and expanded throughout the third and second millennia BC. This formed the basis for further expansion, more intensive agricultural practices and the creation of new types of monumental symbolism in the form of hillforts during the Iron Age.

The Iron Age – Dinedor Camp

By far the most prominent, and obvious, historic monument within the Dinedor area is Dinedor Camp. This impressive earthwork sits upon the highest point of Dinedor Hill, with far reaching views over the surrounding countryside. The name Dinedor is Celtic in origin and means 'fortified hill'. The monument comprises a 'univallate' enclosure, (i.e. with a single bank and ditch or rampart) hillfort of oval shape, the rampart essentially following the natural contours of the hill. The defensive rampart encloses an area of approximately 4 hectares (9.5 acres). Towards the north-east corner of the enclosure, the rampart is at its most impressive and survives to a height of 4.5 metres above the internal level of the hillfort and about 7 metres above the external ground level. These ramparts are the highest in the camp since they face the relatively flat Dinedor Ridge which is the side most susceptible to attack. On its western and northern sides the rampart was made up of stone and earth which was excavated from an external terrace or berm which was approximately 8 metres wide and a broad but shallow, internal quarry ditch. The rampart on the southern and eastern sides was made up of material thrown up from an external defensive ditch. It is likely that the rampart would have been at least partially revetted with dry stone walling in order to stabilise it and would have had a timber pallisade along its top. It had a single entrance at its south-eastern corner which is defended by a bank and ditch outwork.

It is believed that this type of monument began to be constructed over much of Britain shortly after 500BC. Whilst commonly called hillforts and certainly often located on or close to strategically important features and constructed with defence in mind, it is currently thought that these massive earthworks were also designed to be regarded as symbols of power. Such a major earthwork must have been visible for many miles and stood as testament to the strength, power and organisational ability of the social elite who were in charge of a community. Small scale excavation of Dinedor Camp and others in the region (Eaton Bishop and Credenhill) suggests that these defended enclosures were used for a variety of purposes, including markets, social gatherings, storage of crops and other important resources; but were not necessarily permanently lived in by the community. It would appear that the majority of the surrounding population spent most of their lives living in small settlements and farmsteads within the surrounding landscape, only spending time within the hillfort when requested or allowed to do so, or during times of conflict. Herefordshire lies within an area which could have been controlled by either the Silures tribe, which covered an area west of the River Severn and down to the south of Wales or (most likely) the Dubonni which appears to have controlled most of Gloucestershire and the Cotswolds.

The latest date for the Iron Age occupation of Dinedor hillfort appears to be the 2nd century BC. Investigations immediately below the ramparts at the eastern end of the hillfort found middle Iron Age pottery sherds dating from approximately 350 to 100BC as well as some Roman Severn Valley ware indicating occasional occupation after the Iron Age in the Roman period. Current archaeological knowledge suggests that many of these hillforts had fallen into disuse well before the Roman invasion of 47AD. It would appear that huts and other buildings within hillforts were not replaced, the defences were left to fall into disre-pair and the communities which had constructed and maintained them no longer used them on a regular basis. The reasons for this are not fully understood but may well reflect changes within the socio-economic culture of the time. Excavations during the 1950s within the hillfort revealed evidence of post holes for huts, charred grain and flint sickles together with quern stones for grinding cereals. Loom weights were also discovered indicating that wool was being woven into clothing and other products.

The sides of Dinedor Hill immediately below the hillfort have a series of concentric terraces on them. These represent the earthwork remains of an Iron Age field system which was re-used and adapted during the medieval period. Recent surveys of these earthworks

Dinedor Hill as seen from Ridgehill

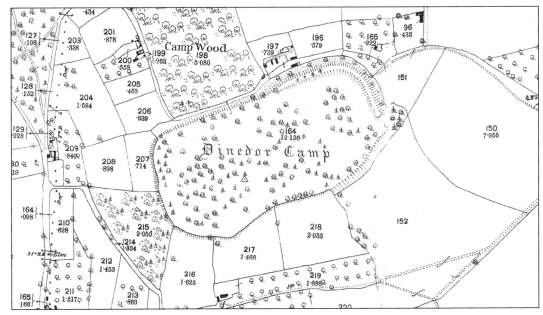

Dinedor Camp and surrounding fields as shown on the 1886 Ordnance Survey Map

have also recorded a track, or hollow way, up to 4 metres wide, leading from the hillfort entrance down the hill in the direction of Hollow Farm. This may have been the original Iron Age route into the hillfort. For more about the terraces see pages 24-25.

The role which the hillfort played in relation to its relationships with other Iron Age enclosures is uncertain. Dinedor Camp is one of 41 hillforts in the county and is about average in size, the smallest (Mere Hill) enclosing no more than a couple of acres whereas the defences of Credenhill, located just to the north-west of Hereford, enclose nearly 50 hectares (120 acres), making it the second largest hillfort in Britain (after Maiden Castle in Dorset). Credenhill is twice as big as any other hillfort in Herefordshire and it is likely to have been the centre of power, or the political capital, in this region during the Iron Age. It is certainly interesting to note that the Romans used the largely abandoned Credenhill hillfort as a supply base from which the engineers and logistical support was used in the construction of the Roman town of *Magnis* (Kenchester).

The population of Iron Age Herefordshire is a subject which has been debated widely. The number of hillforts within the county, together with the huge amount of evidence for field systems and farmsteads, whilst patently not all contemporary, point to a population of many tens of thousands. The sheer amount of time in person hours invested in the construction of even a small hillfort is huge, and could only have been done on a seasonal basis so as to not interfere with the production of crops.

Dinedor Camp is also sometimes known as Oyster Hill. The origins of this name are not known for certain, however the fact that evidence of Romano-British occupation of some areas within the hillfort have been recorded, which includes the presence of oyster shells, (oyster shells are commonly encountered on Roman sites), may have some bearing on the name. Some think the name is connected with that of Ostorius Scapula, (see pages 12 and 176).

Dinedor Camp rampart as shown on a postcard circa *1910. (© Derek Foxton Archives)*

Dinedor Camp, being located in a prominent position and with panoramic views, would have been well placed to control the movement of goods, livestock and people up and down the Wye Valley. In addition, the fact that it is surrounded by well drained slopes and rich soils suggests that the Dinedor and Rotherwas area (like most of the county) was capable of supporting a large and possibly wealthy population. The capability of the region to produce food in large volume, as well as the presence of other important resources nearby (such as iron in the south of the county), would have made Herefordshire an attractive prospect to the incoming Roman regime.

Roman Dinedor

Immediately prior to the Roman invasion and settlement of Britain, Herefordshire appears to have been a relatively heavily populated region centred on agricultural production. There is little evidence to suggest that the 'Romanisation' of Herefordshire was not peaceful, with most of the hillforts having already been deserted, some being used occasionally for ritual ceremonies and as livestock corals. Due to the gradual nature of the Roman settlement, (with the exception of the construction of a military infrastructure to gain better access into Wales), it appears that daily life for the average person changed little. Archaeological excavations of a number of farmsteads across the county have shown that their occupation continued from the Iron Age into the Romano-British period. There is a growing body of evidence to suggest that many farmsteads were expanded into small villa farms, suggesting that the local, if not regional, economy grew during the 2nd and 3rd centuries AD.

Evidence of Roman domestic settlement has been encountered at a number of locations in and around Dinedor and Rotherwas. Excavations associated with the Rotherwas Ribbon and the construction of the new Rotherwas Access Road have unearthed considerable evidence for Romano-British settlement including a possible villa/farmstead site on the northern slope of Dinedor Hill. Romano-British pottery and other artefacts were recovered from excavations undertaken during the 1950s, again suggesting that the now redundant hillfort was being re-used as an enclosure and farmstead. The chance finds of Roman pottery, occasional coins and other artefacts from within the hillfort may well have led to the erroneous assumption by some antiquarians that the hillfort was of Roman military origins. In 1870-72, John Marius Wilson's *Imperial Gazetteer of England and Wales* described Dinedor as: 'Dinedor Hill is crowned by a Roman camp, supposed to be that of Ostorius Scapula.'

This reference appears to have been picked up by other scholars who had clearly not visited the site. *A Chronology of the Roman Empire* by Timothy Venning, and Professor J.F. Drinkwater states that 'in AD50 Ostorius Scapula campaigns against Caratacus on what is now the Mid-Welsh border with new Roman forts being erected in the area including Dinedor Hill near Hereford'.

It is currently believed that Ostorius Scapula moved his troops through northern Herefordshire and southern Shropshire, as suggested by the number of legionary and smaller marching camps and supply depots to the west of Leintwardine. To date no evidence has been found of Roman military installations within Dinedor or Rotherwas.

The archaeological evidence for Romano-British settlement in and around Dinedor fits well with the pattern of settlement covering most of Herefordshire. That is to say a mix of principally agricultural smallholdings and farmsteads interspersed with larger, more Romanised, villa-estates.

The Future

It is clear that the history of continuous human occupation goes back at least to the Neolithic, if not beyond, and extends through the Bronze Age and Iron Age to a period of Romano-British settlement. The common theme across the four millennia or more briefly described within this chapter is the attraction and suitability which the area holds for farming. It is clear that the topography, soils and even localised weather systems have always made the region a prime area for the cultivation of crops and the grazing of livestock.

The development-led archaeological work undertaken over the last decade has highlighted the potential for well-preserved archaeology of regional and national significance. There is great scope for future exploration of the prehistory of Dinedor. Can more be found out about the Rotherwas Ribbon to clarify its purpose? Would excavations in the area of the ridge and the fields below Dinedor Camp hillfort aid an understanding of the early clearance and settlement of Herefordshire? Further investigation to unpick the more recent medieval field systems from earlier Iron Age agricultural remnants and the investigation of the promontory at the end of the ridge are also exciting possibilities for future exploration into our prehistoric past.

3   Landscape Change in Dinedor

by Chris Atkinson, B.A., M.A.

The parish of Dinedor, like every other location within the British Isles has been subjected to continual forces of change. The courses of its streams and rivers, the divisions of its land, its routes of communication, the use of its land, and the focus of settlement have not stood still but evolved. This chapter introduces the landscape changes witnessed within the current extent of the parish of Dinedor.

The Prehistoric Landscape

Archaeological investigations have shed some light on a landscape with no written history. Evidence has been found for settlement upon the raised river gravel terraces of the River Wye from the Mesolithic (9600-4000BC) through to the Mid to Late Bronze Age, including a single pit containing Late Neolithic Flint and Grooved Ware pottery and a Bronze Age roundhouse at the foot of the north face of Dinedor Ridge. The discovery of what has become known as the Rotherwas Ribbon takes the story from the Late Neolithic through to the Bronze Age. Although its purpose is not, and may never be, fully understood, the Ribbon would appear to hold some religious or ceremonial purpose within the landscape, running as it does from the dominant ridgeline of Dinedor Hill to the south and the snaking River Wye to the north and east. It probably formed an important part of a landscape that was both experienced and used in a way that may be alien to us today. (For more on the Ribbon see chapter 2.)

It is during the Bronze Age (2500-750BC) and Iron Age (750BC-43AD) that the earliest and most visibly dominant evidence for prehistoric land use appear, in the form of Dinedor Camp located upon the western end of the Dinedor ridgeline. Although the hillfort, a scheduled monument, has been subject to the most limited of investigations, results of excavations of hillforts across the county and beyond have caused much debate about the role these monuments had within the landscape. At a basic level they represent symbols of power. The ability of an individual or individuals to command a population to construct such monuments can never be underestimated, particularly when that population also needed to be kept fed and watered whilst undertaking the everyday agricultural, industrial and trading tasks that all required manual labour. The location of these sites at prominent places within the landscape meant not only that these symbols of power could be observed from great distances by visitors and locals alike, but also that the territory that the tribal leader commanded could be observed from the hilltop site.

Apart from the location of hillforts and individual settlements, our knowledge of the way in which the landscape was organised and used during this time is limited. However, by the end of the Bronze Age and into the Iron Age deforestation of the region would certainly have been in full swing, both to clear land for agricultural use and to provide fuel and building materials.

The Roman Landscape

Our first historical reference to the region in which Dinedor lies comes from the writings of Tacitus, who describes the campaigns against the tribes of Britain, in particular the tribal leader Caratacus following the Roman Invasion in 43AD. By 47AD the Roman Army had reached Herefordshire and established a military frontier within the territory of the Dobunni, a confederation of tribes that covered an area from mid Herefordshire (including Dinedor) into Worcestershire and Gloucestershire. Excavations between 2007 and 2009 at the Iron Age hillfort of Credenhill, located a few miles to north of Dinedor Camp, identified the presence of Roman material and structures, indicating the military's use of the site as a likely supply base during the conquest period. This is a pattern of re-use similar to a site south of the village of Leintwardine in the north of Herefordshire, where the hillfort of Brandon Camp was utilised by the Roman army on their arrival in the area. Unlike the area around Brandon Camp however, no associated Roman marching camps or forts have yet been identified in the vicinity of Credenhill.

With the arrival of the Roman army came the construction of roads to link the major military sites. Dated to the reign of the Emperor Nero, the main north-south route known as Watling Street West extended from Chester south through the legionary fortress at Wroxeter to the auxiliary fort at Leintwardine and on to the foot of Credenhill hillfort. From here it crossed the River Wye and continued south until reaching the legionary fortress of Usk.[1] Extending westwards from this main artery were a series of other roads that led to forts situated at the foot of the Welsh highlands. One such road led from Kenchester to the west of Credenhill to cross the Wye and head to Clyro and Clifford, sites of forts within the vicinity of Hay-on-Wye, and also headed east from Kenchester to Worcester. The resulting crossroads, with its close proximity to the River Wye crossing and set in the heart of fertile lands, would have been busy not just with the movement of the army, but also of military supplies, officials, merchants, and also with local inhabitants looking to trade their wares. This in turn helped promote the growth of a town (*Magnis*) during the late first and second centuries AD.

Today nothing is visible of the town except for a short stretch of wall within a modern hedgerow, the relic of a defensive wall that encompassed the site between the 3rd and 5th centuries. In suitable conditions, however, it is possible through aerial photography to pick out the now buried course of the main road that once extended west towards Wales (Figure 1).

In the case of Dinedor there is no evidence to suggest a direct Roman military presence, neither is it known that any substantial settlement then existed within the modern extent of the parish. Recent excavations within the parishes of Dinedor and Lower Bullingham, resulting from the recent development of the Rotherwas Enterprise Zone and modern housing, has, however, identified a Romano-British rural landscape. It is clear that the

*Figure 1: Aerial photograph taken in the summer of 2013 showing the course of the
Roman Road running through the Roman town of Magnis
(© Community Heritage and Archaeology Consultancy)*

fertile alluvial soils and gravel terraces were just as appealing to the farmer then as they
are today. Excavations have identified multiple ditched land divisions, presumably once
associated with raised banks and hedgerows. The presence of Romano-British pottery of a
reasonable status plus the discovery of a metalled Roman surface at the foot of Dinedor Hill
also indicate the presence of a substantial farmstead within the vicinity.

The British and Saxon Landscape

Although the Parish of Dinedor now lies firmly within the borders of England, following
the Roman abandonment of *Britannia* the region initially formed part of the British (Welsh)
kingdom of Glywising (Gwent). The region, however, quickly became a hotbed of military
turbulence, with the numerous British households, the invading Saxons and raiding Danes
all vying for territorial gains.

> Be it known that great tribulations and plunderings happened in the time of Teithfallt
> and Ithael, Kings of Wales, which were committed by the most treacherous Saxon
> nation, and principally on the borders of Wales and England, towards Hereford, so that
> all the border country of Wales was nearly destroyed, and much beyond the borders
> in both England and Wales, and especially about the river Wye, on account of the
> frequent diurnal and nocturnal encounters which took place between both countries.

After a time, peace being established, the land was restored to its owners and its former authority, although destroyed and depopulated by foreign people, and an uncommon pestilence, and an alliance of the Britons formed in those parts.[2]

By the early 7th century a new British kingdom, known as Ergyng, had emerged that extended from Monmouthshire, beyond the River Wye, into Herefordshire and south into Gloucestershire and towards the River Severn following a series of victories against the Saxons.

Be it well known to all who dwell in the southern part of Britain, that Gwrfodw King of Ergyng, having gained a victory in battle over the Saxon nation, and giving thanks to God and for the prayers of Bishop Ufelwy, and his clergy, granted in alms to him, and all his successors, under the refuge of St. Dubricius, and St. Teilo, forever, the land called Bolgros [Preston on Wye], on the banks of the Wye, at some distance from Mochros [Moccas], of the quantity of three uncias [approximately 324 acres]. And the land having been given as an endowment, Bishop Ufelwy, with his clergy, went round the whole of its boundary, sprinkling holy water, the holy cross with the holy relics being carried before; and in the presence of the King, with his witnesses, built a church in the middle thereof …[3]

Although the information is sketchy, by the end of the 9th century it seems the union between the Saxon kingdoms of Mercia and Wessex led to the conquest and amalgamation of much of the British (Welsh) northern territory of Ergyng into the territory of Mercia. The Parker version of the Anglo Saxon Chronicle states:

In this year [853AD] Burhred, King of Mercia, and his councillors besought King Æthelwulf that he would help them to subject the Welsh. He then did so, and with his levies went through Mercia into Wales, and they made them all obedient to them.[4]

What remained of Ergyng was recognised as Archenfield by the Saxons, under whom the territory became a semi-autonomous Welsh territory outside of Saxon law. The border between the two territories lay along the course of the current parish boundary formed by the Tar's Brook, the Worm Brook to the west of Aconbury and beyond along the River Dore. The conquered area in which Dinedor is located became known as Dunre and for a time was administered by the 'common burdens' exacted upon the population by Mercian overlord kings, which included military service, the upkeep of roads and bridges, as well as fortress work.[5] It was in the mid 10th century, during the rule of King Athelstan, that the Shires and Hundreds of England became the basis for administration.[6] Each Shire consisted of a number of Hundreds each of which was subdivided into 100 hides, a hide representing an area of land suitable for sustaining a single, albeit extended, peasant family.

Each Hundred became the key unit of local administration, taxation and justice in which a court was held once a month where disputes could be settled, new laws read out and property titles established. It is likely that the Hundred of Dunre emerged at this date, its name perhaps deriving from a meeting place for the court on Dinedor Hill. The Hundred was, however, considerably larger than the modern parish, as is evident from the Domesday

Survey of 1086 in which it includes the manors not just of Dinedor, but also Barton, Bullinghope, Cobhall, Rotherwas, Holme Lacy and Webton.

What survives of this post-Roman pre-Norman landscape within Dinedor today? The most obvious survivor is perhaps the name. Dinedor derives the British/Welsh *Din* meaning 'fort' and *Bre* meaning 'hill', which evolved to become Dunre once the region came under Saxon control.[7] Through further evolution the name gradually transformed to what we recognise today.

Beyond the name, it is clear that the southern extent of the parish, the course of the Tar's Brook, continued to represent an important political boundary as not only did it mark the border between Archenfield and Dunre but, until 1133, during the reign of Bishop Urban, it continued to mark the north-eastern extent of the Diocese of Llandaff.

> The boundaries of the diocese of Llandaff are the following: From the mouth of Towy at the sea, upwards as far as its source, then to Pendeu-lwynhelig, to Blaenwysc, to the Black Mountain, … along it to the Gwormwy, along it to its source, then to Caer Rein [thought to be the hillfort of Aconbury], to the source of the Taratyr [Tar's Brook], along it to the River Wye, and along the River Wye to the Severn sea, thence to the mouth of the river Towy, where the diocese of Llandaff begins.[8]

When it comes to details of field systems across the parish or even of settlements prior to the evidence provided by the Domesday Survey, we find ourselves a little stuck, principally because of continued and occasionally intensive use of the land over the subsequent centuries. It is generally thought that between the abandonment of Britain by the Romans and the late Saxon period (*c.*9th century), the population of the British Isles was not large enough to warrant the intensive and extensive exploitation of the land through the process of mass enclosure and deforestation. As a result, agrarian society probably continued to employ the fields established during the period of Roman occupation, but preferred to avoid the heavier clay soils in favour of lighter free draining areas such as river terrace gravels.[9]

If this was the case, it would seem reasonable to suggest that early medieval society, whether British or Saxon, would have focused on the cultivation of the multiple terraces of the River Wye left behind following the last glacial period. Elsewhere, the flood plains would have been ideal for pasture and meadows, whereas the marginal upland areas such as the Dinedor ridgeline would have been dominated by woodland. Certainly, by the time of the Norman Conquest in 1066, two of the manors of Dunre (Dinedor and Barton) had woodland held by King William himself, whereas the manors of Boninhope (Bullinghope) and Boniniope (another Bullinghope) lay within the extensive royal forest of Haye.

Despite the lack of visual evidence, it is believed that as part of the administrative reforms of the 10th century a form of open-field farming was being established across southern England, in which peasant farmers communally farmed, as part of the Hundred system, strips of unenclosed, open land which included arable, pasture and meadow.[10] The act of creating these large open fields would have had a marked effect on any pre-existing forms of land division as, by its very nature, the open field did not contain laid hedges or bank and ditch boundaries. As such, 10th-century land reform would have involved considerable clearance of landscape features.

The Medieval Landscape

Dinedor's Manors

It is with the Norman Conquest, in particular the audit of the counties of England commissioned and directed by King William I and completed by 1086, that our first detailed account for the lands of Dinedor and its population can be found.

The Hundred of Dunre was considerably larger than the parish appears today, containing the settlements of Dinedor, Barton, Cobhall, Rotherwas, Lower Bullingham, Bullinghope, Mawfield, Webton, Holme Lacy and a since vanished second settlement of Bullinghope. Of these settlements, Dinedor and Rotherwas lie within the modern bounds of the parish.

At the time of the 1086 survey Dunre was owned by Ralph of Tosny:

> William and his brother Ilbert hold from him. Godric and Wulfheah held it as two manors. 6 hides which pay tax. In lordship 2 ploughs; 13 villagers with a reeve and 5 smallholders with 12 ploughs. 4 ploughmen and 3 female slaves. A mill at 28d; the King has the woodland of this [manor] in lordship. No-one fishes in the river without permission. Value of these two manors before 1066 £7 5s; now the same.[11]

Retrowas (Rotherwas) was owned and held by Gilbert son of Thorold:

> Sigric held it before 1066. 3 hides which pay tax. In lordship 2 ploughs; 2 villagers and 3 smallholders with 2 ploughs. Value before 1066 £6; now £3. There were 10 villagers with 13 ploughs.[12]

Of particular interest is the reference to the value of each manor prior to the Norman Conquest. Clearly Dinedor was the more successful of the two settlements as between 1066 and 1086 Rotherwas had greatly declined in size, having previously supported a population of 10 villagers (each villager representing a peasant family with the most land; below them in the feudal scale came smallholders and then cottagers) with 13 ploughs (a plough representing eight oxen and not just the plough itself) with a value of £6. By 1086 the settlement had halved in value and its population dropped to only 2 villagers and 3 smallholders.

Dinedor, in comparison, had a Reeve (a manor official elected by the peasantry who would oversee the running of a settlement including its agricultural activity), 13 villagers, 5 smallholders, 4 ploughmen and 3 female slaves (a slave was someone who owed a personal service to someone else and was unable to move, change work or buy or sell land, without permission). Not counting the slaves or the lord of the manor this would suggest that 23 households were associated with Dinedor, while Rotherwas only numbered 5 households by 1086.

Even armed with this information it is difficult to assess the total population due to the fact that Domesday only counted the head of each household rather than the number of people that made up each household. It is only with the Poll Tax of 1379 that we are able to gain a sense of the size of each of the settlements in question. Each lay, married or single man and woman over the age of 16 was assessed for taxes, which, depending on their social status and moveable goods (such as crops and livestock), would range between 4d and 10 marks (£6 13 shillings and 4 pence).[13] Within Dinedor 26 individuals were subject to tax, but within Rotherwas the number totalled 29. Rotherwas remained the poorer neighbour to Dinedor however as none of the population were taxed above 4d (total revenue of 9s 8d) which might suggest the population consisted of peasant labourers. On the other hand, the tax raised from Dinedor amounted to 10 shillings[14] and the settlement included two craftsmen, two tailors and a rope/net maker.

With the exception of the 13th-century church of St Andrew's in the village of Dinedor, today's visitor may be forgiven for not knowing that both in Dinedor and the bustling industrial zone of Rotherwas there were once medieval villages. In the case of Rotherwas the village is thought to have lain within the grounds of the later Rotherwas House, seat of the Bodenham Family from 1483. Nothing is known of the form of the village with the exception that it was situated along a lane (now a minor farm track) that once extended from the Wye at Lower Bullingham, eastwards to the site of the then village. The lane then ran south-east around the foot of the eastern end of the Dinedor ridgeline from where it crossed and then continued following the course of the river to Ross-on-Wye via the village of Fownhope (Figure 2).

In Dinedor, the church of St Andrew's is located at the end of a green lane that extends south from the crossroads within the modern village. The surrounding buildings have their origins in structures that date from the 1600s at the earliest. So does the original medieval village lie beneath these buildings, or elsewhere? The 'main' road that forms one arm of the crossroads traverses the southern foot of the Dinedor ridgeline to link with the 'old'

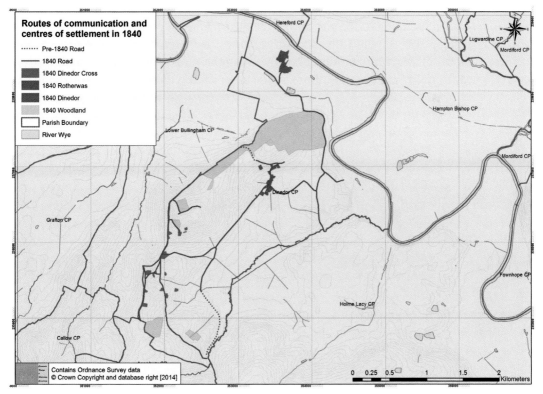

Figure 2: A map showing the location of settlements and the developing network of roads
(© Community Heritage and Archaeology Consultancy)

Ross-on-Wye road (via Holme Lacy and Fownhope) to the east, and to the west with a lane linking Hereford and Ross-on-Wye (via Much Dewchurch). From the crossroads a lane heads uphill to serve a number of cottages and a farm to the north before it terminates. Originally this lane crossed the summit of the ridge and continued down the far side to link with the current course of Watery Lane that leads past Watery Lane Farm in Lower Bullingham before heading on to Hereford (Figure 2). On the opposite side of the road at the crossroads in Dinedor is a green lane that extends south into Garrison Meadow next to the church. It could be argued that both the green lane and the Dinedor ridge top lane represent the earliest route of communication through the village, rather than the modern road. As such the village may have been stretched along the lane on a north-south axis rather than the predominantly east-west axis as is currently the case. Indeed Garrison Meadow has long been suspected to be the site of a shrunken medieval village and is a Scheduled Monument (No.HE224).

As part of the Dinedor Origins Project, members and volunteers of the Dinedor Heritage Group led a survey and excavation of Garrison Meadow. The field has been under pasture since at least the mid 19th century and almost certainly longer from the multiple lumps and bumps it contains, relics of previous land use. One aim of the excavation was to identify any structures relating to medieval settlement. Though restricted in scope, the excavations found the foundations of a large linear structure with substantial stone foundations and a hearth partially enclosed by a stone wall, both of which suggest that the building belonged to somebody of relatively high status.[15] Despite the limited datable material uncovered due to the intensive landscaping of the site during the post-medieval period, fragments of medieval pottery (dated between the 13th and 14th centuries) were retrieved from across the site. One fragment of B1 Malvernian Ware dated between the mid-13th and early-14th century was retrieved from the remains of a floor surface associated with the hearth (Figure 5).[16]

Figure 3: Aerial view of the lower part of Dinedor village, with the 'lumps and bumps' in Garrison Meadow being clearly seen in the centre of the photograph

Despite the positive results of this excavation, no evidence for the early medieval settlement was uncovered. Thus the question remains as to how the two villages of Dinedor and Rotherwas were organised at the time of the Norman Conquest: were they nucleated around a centre, or were they dispersed, with individual farmsteads scattered amongst the fields of the Dunre Hundred?

Figure 4: The excavation under way on Garrison Meadow in 2013

Woods and Fields

In terms of the general use and organisation of the landscape following the Norman Conquest, further information can be obtained from the references made to the number of ploughs present at each location, as well as the presence of woodland and mills. It is likely that the topographic dominance of the Dinedor ridgeline provided the boundary between Rotherwas and Dinedor. It is likely that the current extensive woodland upon the summit of the ridge and its north-facing slopes (Rotherwas Park Wood) represents the site of the woodland held in Dinedor by the king at the time of the 1086 survey due to its location upon steep, marginal land unsuited to cultivation.

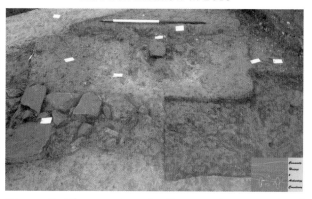

Figure 5: The remains of a floor surface associated with a hearth found in the large linear structure excavated on Garrison Meadow (© Community Heritage and Archaeology Consultancy)

Though held by the king, the woodland is likely to have been maintained by the Tenant-in-Chief, Ralph of Tosny, who delegated its control to the lords of the manor, William and Ilbert. They would have ensured the woodland was not over grazed by anyone who held common rights or timber extracted by anyone without permission to do so, for woodlands were tightly regulated resources in the Norman period and often enclosed by substantial boundaries consisting of a bank and ditch accompanied by a hedge or fence. The trees were probably pollarded rather than coppiced so as to avoid new growth being grazed by livestock, the peasantry with rights being able to extract the felled boughs whilst the tree's bollings (the pollarded stumps) were retained by the lord of the manor.[17]

When considering the number of villagers and ploughs in the Domesday Survey, the smaller population in Rotherwas and the presence of only 6 ploughs suggests that the primary agrarian concern was that of providing pasture and meadow for livestock grazing and the production of hay for fodder rather than crop cultivation. Indeed, the name

Rotherwas is an indicator of such land use as it probably derives from the Old English *hryther* meaning cattle and *waesse*, a west-midlands place-name for land by a major river (in this case the River Wye) liable to sudden flooding.[18]

In comparison, Dinedor and its 23 households with 14 ploughs would indicate a community far more focused on the cultivation of crops, albeit with the land immediately alongside the banks of the River Wye and the Tar's Brook, as areas prone to flooding, being more suited as meadows and pasture.

Much of the landscape would have continued to have been farmed in the manner of the open-field system established during the reign of King Athelstan. Although the details of this system fluctuated from settlement to settlement, most villages would have had two or three large open unhedged fields divided into strips that were farmed by individual tenants or landowners. In order to sustain the fertility of the soil, each furlong (an individual strip of land within an open field) was farmed in rotation, with the winter crops and spring crops being followed by a period of fallow.[19]

It is the Tithe Map of 1840 that provides us with the visible clues as to how this early medieval landscape may have been laid out. In particular, it helps us to identify the potential location for each of the open fields established in this period. Even in 1840 individual strips of land, the vestiges of the medieval open-field system, continued to be farmed by tenants and owners. In other locations, such as in the west of the parish, small irregularly enclosed fields are present which appear to represent the enclosing or assarting of individual strips

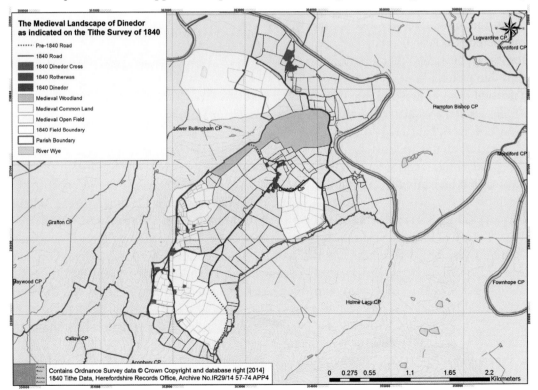

Figure 6: The medieval landscape of Dinedor as indicated by the 1840 Tithe Survey
(© Community Heritage and Archaeology Consultancy)

22

from the open fields by wealthier landowners to create additional arable land (Figure 6). The overall size of these open fields is, however, a little harder to determine due to the extent to which the landscape has been subject to large-scale planned enclosure since the medieval period that has resulted in the removal of any earlier boundaries. Nevertheless, some extensive, sinuous boundaries do survive across the parish, linking with roadways and lanes which are likely to have also played some part in delineating each open field.

With some confidence, three areas of open fields can be identified through observations of the 1840 Tithe Map: one to the west of Rotherwas (which extends into the neighbouring parish of Lower Bullingham), one to the south of Dinedor and another within the vicinity of Dinedor Cross in the west of the parish (Figure 6).

As part of the Dinedor Heritage Group's excavations on Garrison Meadow, a series of test pits were dug, focusing on features identified as a result of the measured survey. These features were interpreted as representing small irregularly enclosed fields extending south-east from the lane. Although this interpretation cannot yet be proven, a soil horizon was visible within all of the trenches which included pottery dating to between the mid-13th and 15th century.[20] As a result of soil analysis, this horizon appears to represent the artificial enrichment of the soils, indicating deliberate manuring of the fields, between the 13th and 15th centuries. The physical presence of the pottery may indicate the spreading of household waste as a fertiliser.[21]

The Waste of the Manor

It is at this point that the role of Dinedor Common and Dinedor Cross Common must be considered. Common land, as we know it today, was referred to as waste at the time of Domesday. Such waste consisted of land deemed unprofitable for agricultural improvement due primarily to its topographical location and the fertility of the soil. The majority of present day commons are therefore found upon steep slopes and hills or within areas of marsh or boggy ground. In the case of Dinedor, there are two commons: Dinedor Common, located upon the steep western face of Dinedor Hill, and Dinedor Cross Common, both locations being upon the higher ground in the west.

What is of particular interest, however, is that there is no reference to waste within the Hundred of Dunre in the Domesday Survey, with the exception of Barton. This would suggest that Dinedor Common and Dinedor Cross Common are later additions to the historic landscape. It is also thought, as recounted earlier, that the summit and slopes of Dinedor were covered in woodland at the time of the survey and, to the west, this may have adjoined the expanse of the royal forest of Haye, which is known to have begun:

> ... at the bridge of the Wey [Wye] ... within the town of Hereford and thus by descending through the town of Potestone [Putson] which is now in the forest, and as far as the main road through the middle of the said town from the surrounding countryside by a kind of de la Calewe [The Callow] even to the cross at the head of the same town and of the said mill ventrium outside of the town of Dewyswelle And about the same as far as the mill as far as Kivernowesbrugge And from that day to the place which is called the Stockwell And then by means of the royal and as far as the place that is called the way of and then to the village of Hundirton [Hunderton] by including all the whole towne Welbetre [Webtree] arrive at the bridge of the Waya [Wye]).[22]

The eastern edge of the Haye between Putson and Callow would have taken it close to the foot of Dinedor Hill. Therefore, for the common land to be established, either the woodland referred to as being located within the manor of Dinedor in 1086 was removed, or the woodland contracted in size, perhaps due to poor management.

The nature of the enclosures upon this area of the hill, as well as the results of a recent light detection and ranging (LIDAR) survey carried out by the Environment Agency (Figure 7), support the first theory of the woodland having been removed. By the end of the 13th century the population of England had risen sharply to between 5 and 6 million people. This resulted in the need for more cultivable soils, as the land long since farmed was becoming exhausted of the nutrients and minerals needed for a successful harvest. To compound the problem, towards the end of the 13th century there was a deterioration in the climate which came to a climax in the early 14th century (in particular between 1315-17), causing harvests to fail or produce diseased crops.[23] As a result, both the human and livestock populations were malnourished and more prone to disease.

Within Herefordshire, it is thought that the population at this point numbered around 100,000 people, requiring both the peasantry and the aristocracy to acquire new lands for food and fodder production. This led to the cultivation of land that would otherwise be regarded as marginal, attention in Dinedor turning towards the steep south- and west-facing slopes of the Dinedor ridgeline. As part of the Dinedor Origins Project, aerial photographs, field survey and LIDAR have all aided in the mapping of strip linear agricultural terraces (lynchets) that traverse these steep slopes (Figure 7). The creation of these terraces would have been no easy task, and would have absorbed considerable resources and time for what may only have been a limited crop gain due to the poor climate and general lack of quality fertiliser provided by a malnourished and diseased livestock. Writing between 1316 and 1317, chronicler Henry Knighton of Leicester described the situation at its worst:

> There was a horrific mortality of humans and a pestilence of animals throughout the kingdom of England; conditions were so bad that the surviving people did not have the wherewithal to cultivate or sow their lands, and every day they were burying as many as they could in improvised cemeteries.[24]

The lynchets in question were most probably constructed during the early stages of what became known as the Great Famine in the late 13th century. Thus a large proportion of the royal forest was sacrificed to the need for food, with the likely exception of an area of woodland upon the eastern end of the ridge which appears to have been retained due to the absence of any evidence of lynchets being found there. Although the lynchets that have been found on the south- and west-facing slopes await the excavations of an archaeologist, it is probable that the steep slopes were sculpted by the creation of a series of parallel timber or stone retaining walls, up slope of which earth was piled to create the surface on which fertiliser would be added and then seeds sown and managed as an extension of the open-field system.

It is because of the location of the lynchets upon the steep slopes that they survive intact to this day. Not even with the expansion of agriculture during the Second World War did the Dinedor ridgeline witness as intensive cultivation as during this period of the medieval

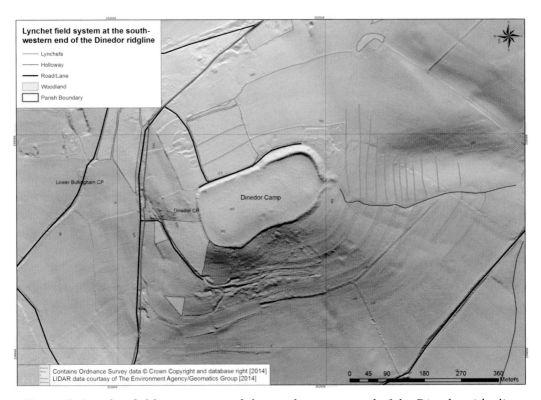

Figure 7: Lynchet field system around the south-western end of the Dinedor ridgeline
(© Community Heritage and Archaeology Consultancy)

era. The most physically striking area of lynchets survives upon the south-facing slope of ridge, immediately beneath Dinedor Camp. Both from field survey and the available LIDAR coverage, it is possible to identify two distinct areas of lynchets divided by a holloway/ boundary that may represent the original route way into the Bronze/Iron Age hillfort. The lynchets to the east of the hollow are much narrower and appear to have extended further east along the hillside beyond the bounds of the current field. In comparison, those to the west appear much broader in size but, like those to the east, extend westwards to encompass the end of Dinedor Hill. The LIDAR coverage also suggests they may have extended continuously around the north face of the ridge, where they are preserved within Camp Wood (Figure 7). Of particular interest is the relationship between this series of lynchets and the hollow that extends downslope from the entrance to Dinedor Camp. Not only are they broader in construction than those to the east, but they also appear to infringe upon and terminate within the hollow. Further work needs to be done to disentangle the relationship between the features as it is known that during the first half of the 19th century some cultivation was carried out upon the earlier lynchets within the field in question. As a result, the extension of the lynchets into the holloway from the west may be the result of 19th-century activity.

Following the disaster that was the Great Famine, and then the catastrophe of the Black Death that reached England in May 1348, the crash in population numbers would have led to the relatively quick abandonment of these upland marginal terraced fields, and a return in focus to the more freely available, fertile and easily cultivable alluvial soils on the plains. It is at this point that Dinedor Common may have come into existence as waste, and common-rights awarded to specific families by order of the lord of the manor of Dinedor due to the land now being regarded as of low worth. The presence of both Camp Wood and Little Camp Wood upon the hill is testament to the re-establishment of woodland on the hill following the abandonment of the fields, and it can only be assumed that the two areas as they stand today were once joined and likely to have extended across into Dinedor Camp. Due to their close proximity, both Dinedor Common and Dinedor Cross Common are likely to have represented a single area of waste from the mid 14th century.

The Park

By the late 15th century the landscape of Dinedor was transformed once more with the establishment of Rotherwas Park. The event occurred with the passing of the Rotherwas Manor by marriage from the de la Barre family to the Bodenhams in 1483. The park extended south from Rotherwas House to encompass the vestiges of the King's Wood upon the eastern end of Dinedor Hill, today known as Rotherwas Park Wood. The full extent of the park is difficult to judge today, but field name evidence provided by the Tithe Apportionment of 1842[25] provides some indications. Surrounding Rotherwas Park Wood are fields under arable known as Park Field, Lower Park Field and Upper Park Field, as well as fields under pasture known as Upper Park Lawns and Lower Park Lawns (Figure 8).

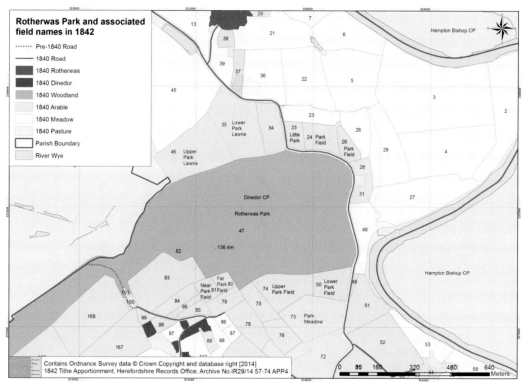

Figure 8: Rotherwas Park and associated field names in 1842
(© Community Heritage and Archaeology Consultancy)

Early parks were not the ornamental gardens and expanses that we might recognise today but were instead managed for the rearing of deer. As a result a park pale consisting of an internal ditch and external bank with either a hedge or palisade on its summit was constructed as a means of preventing the farmed deer from entering the surrounding arable fields.[26] The establishment of a park did not necessarily mean the displacement of the people who farmed the land prior to its establishment, for where open-fields existed their use often continued. This may explain why so many small irregular fields (enclosed as a result of wealthy farmers undertaking assarting) existed in the area around Rotherwas Park Wood in 1842.

The Post-Medieval and Modern Landscape

Enclosing an Open and Waste Landscape
The current layout of the parish owes much to the changes in agricultural practice from the 17th century through to the modern day. Our understanding of this changing layout and use of the landscape is made considerably easier than for earlier periods due to the available literature and historic map data.

It is the Tithe Map of 1840 that provides us with our first detailed visual representation as to how the landscape was organised in the past. As well as being able to identify the scattered fossilised remains of a once open medieval landscape, the observer is drawn to both the small and larger rectangular and irregularly planned field enclosures.

It is the smaller, irregularly shaped fields upon the western end of the Dinedor ridgeline as well as around Dinedor Cross that are likely to be the results of some of the earliest acts of enclosure within the parish. The process of assarting was usually driven by population and financial pressures.[27] In the case of Dinedor, the underlying lynchets identified across the hillsides and beneath the small enclosures in question would suggest that assarting did not occur until after the Great Famine of the late 13th and early 14th century, with an increase in activity during the post-medieval period.

The piecemeal assarting of the common land in Dinedor over time was undertaken by individual farmers looking to invest in land and in certain instances establish a farmstead or household away from the main settlements. It is most likely for this reason that the hamlet of Dinedor Cross came into existence, as numerous farmers encroached, claimed and cleared areas of the once wooded common land, the vestiges of which survive in the form of Camp Wood, Little Camp Wood and Dinedor Common.

There has been much discussion about the origins and reasoning behind the appearance of the much larger field enclosures. As with all land reforms it is thought to be due to a mixture of population, financial and technological factors. By the 17th century the population is believed to have regained the levels present in England before the Great Famine and Black Death, resulting in the need for increased food production. It was the introduction of new agricultural techniques that led to the irregular enclosure of large areas of the open-field systems around the settlements of both Dinedor and Rotherwas, as well as to the south of Dinedor Cross. Groups of arable strip fields were amalgamated and subsequently enclosed, the land then being taken out of cultivation and reverting to grass pasture for a number of years allowing for soil fertility to improve (Figure 9). In the meantime areas of land once used for pasture were used to grow arable crops.

27

Trying to gauge an accurate idea of the size of population during this period is difficult, until you reach the latter half of the 17th century and the advent of assessments for the Hearth Tax between 1662 and 1689. There are a number of factors to keep in mind when using this record however. Firstly, the Hearth Tax Assessment is only concerned with households who lived in houses with chimneys and therefore hearths – the more chimneys located within a property, the more tax one would pay. As a result the assessment ignores those households that did not possess chimneys, which is thought to represent about 40% of households across Herefordshire.[28] Secondly, the record is not interested in taking note of the number of people resident within each household, only listing the individual at its head. That aside, the Michaelmas Hearth Tax Assessment of 1665 indicates that across the parish there were 38 chargeable hearths located across 15 households. Rotherwas House headed the list with 14 chargeable hearths, followed by Dinedor Court with 5.[29] If we consider that 40% of households were excluded from the assessment, this would suggest that there were 25 households within the parish. To obtain the parish's population, a multiplier of between 4.3 and 4.5 is believed to give a fairly accurate figure from this hearth assessment, meaning a population of *circa* 110.

It was with the 18th century that the planned rectangular field enclosures visible on the Tithe Map that extend south from the summit of the Dinedor ridgeline towards the Tar's Brook first appear. Elsewhere these enclosures are evident upon the floodplains adjacent to the River Wye, and by the later 19th century (as evident in the 1881 First County Series

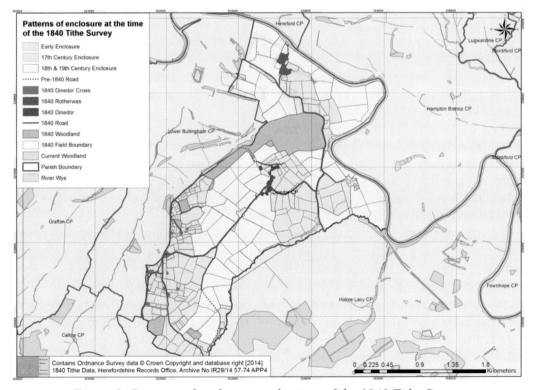

Figure 9: Patterns of enclosure at the time of the 1840 Tithe Survey
(© Community Heritage and Archaeology Consultancy)

Survey) to the south and south-east of Dinedor village, where the enclosures made upon the open-field system in the 17th and 18th centuries were further amalgamated.

The process of creating these enclosures involved the total reorganisation into a system that no longer resembled nor necessarily preserved the evidence for earlier patterns of field enclosure. It was during the agricultural revolution that the age of parliamentary enclosure was born. New ploughs, drills, threshing machines and reapers were introduced, and there was an increase in the sowing of clovers and grasses for the enhancement of soil fertility. Similarly the cultivating of root crops such as potatoes and turnips became extensive.[30]

The parliamentary Enclosure Acts caused much resentment amongst rural populations. Livelihoods, once centred upon the common fields, were being uprooted as land ownership became concentrated in the hands of the wealthiest farmers. This in turn led to a general decrease in rural population as families emigrated to towns and cities to seek employment in the ever increasing numbers of industrial factories.

Apart from the argument that enclosure was the only way to ensure the production of a larger harvest from that generated by the medieval open-field system, much of the impetus behind the rate of enclosure lay in the cost of grain. Throughout the 18th and 19th centuries Britain had been in an almost constant state of war, particularly against France, and needed a secure home grown supply of food to feed not just the expanding civilian population, but also the army and the navy. As a result the price of grain was increasing. This in turn encouraged commercially-minded farmers to seek parliamentary enclosure as a means of enhancing their wealth.[31]

New Routes of Communication and Industry

Not only was the landscape undergoing transformation through enclosure, but new field divisions were being formed as a result of improvements to the road network and the construction of railways (along with canals elsewhere in the country). The first 1:2500 Country Series Survey of 1881 shows that the lane serving Rotherwas had been replaced by the 'straight mile' and that the ridge-top lane linking Watery Lane with Dinedor was well and truly gone. In the south of the parish the lane linking Dinedor Cross with the mill on the Tar's Brook had also diminished in length (Figure 10). In 1855 the Hereford and Gloucester Branch of the Great Western Railway was constructed (and decommissioned in 1964) (Figure 10).

With the sale of the Bodenham Estate at Rotherwas in 1912 and the onset of the First World War in 1914, the parishes of Dinedor and neighbouring Lower Bullingham underwent irreversible changes to their landscape. No longer were the parishes purely hubs for small, rural, agrarian communities but the landscape north of the Dinedor ridgeline became a centre for the armaments industry. By 11th November 1916, Rotherwas had become the site of an extensive National Filling Factory, at which the ordnance required on the war front was filled. This was an industry that continued into and beyond the Second World War until it was decommissioned in 1967. With the construction of the factory almost all of the individual field enclosures surrounding Rotherwas disappeared.

Interestingly, despite the introduction of large-scale industry into Dinedor parish during the First World War, census records do not indicate an increase in the size of the population;

29

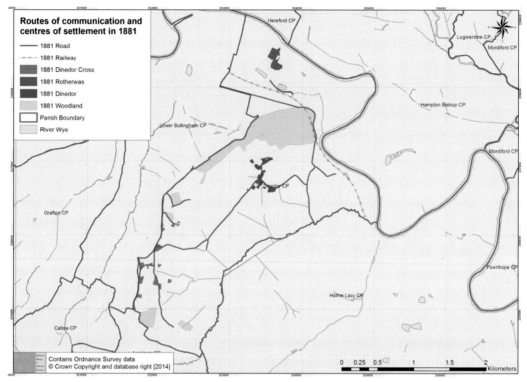

Figure 10: Routes of communication and centres of settlement in 1881
(© Community Heritage and Archaeology Consultancy)

if anything there was a gradual decline during the war periods. In regards to location, the majority of the population continued to live where they do today, primarily clustered within Dinedor village and Dinedor Cross. In 1841 the population across the parish numbered 289; in 1881, 263; in 1901, 225; in 1921, 220; with an increase to 260 in 1961.[32]

Today the munitions factory site remains a hive of activity, having been converted for use as an industrial estate known as the Rotherwas Enterprise Zone. As a result the landscape continues to change as the site grows and requires new land for the construction of new buildings and roads. The building of the Rotherwas Access Road divided and reshaped a number of fields established over a long history, and has perhaps inadvertently created a physical boundary marking the southernmost extent of modern Hereford. Up until its construction this was marked by the course of the London and North Western Railway. In a world once more under pressure from an increased population with the need for affordable housing and resources, the fields now situated between the railway and road are the likely target for further change.

In all of this however, the Dinedor ridgeline continues to maintain its dominance in the parish. It acts as a boundary separating an industrial north from a rural south in which pasture for cattle and sheep and cultivation for cereal crops continues amongst a population scattered amongst farms and cottages, Dinedor Manor, the village of Dinedor and the hamlet of Dinedor Cross.

4 Rotherwas House

by Chris Over

Scattered throughout Herefordshire are the sites and remains of many large country houses that once dominated their immediate surroundings. At their height they provided employment and housing locally, combined with agricultural expertise that served a wider community. The upkeep of these houses in due course proved to be very onerous which meant that when times got difficult several fell prey to unchecked deterioration and ended up being demolished. Some of the more notable in the county that befell such a fate include Harewood House, Garnstone Castle, Goodrich Court and Foxley. Then there was Stoke Edith, which experienced a devastating fire around 1926. These fine old houses now live on largely in ancient prints, although also within the living memory of a rapidly declining number of individuals. The subject of this chapter is one such house, Rotherwas House, of which very little trace remains.

The name Rotherwas is likely to derive from the old English *hryther* meaning cattle, and *waesse,* a west-midlands place-name for land by a major river that was liable to sudden flooding.[1] To most citizens of Herefordshire today the name means a place of industry and employment, factories large and small, traffic queues and the council waste tip; but go back 150 years and the name Rotherwas would conjure up a picture of a large mansion surrounded by parkland with beautiful views of the surrounding countryside.

As in the case of many of the old estates we have to go back to the Domesday Survey of 1086 to trace the origins of Rotherwas House and its estate. At that time Rotherwas (then called Retrowas) was owned by Gilbert, son of Thorold;[2] previously the manor had been held by Sigeric. Gilbert held three hides of land (approx. 360 acres) on which he had to pay tax. He also had two ploughs (in lordship) and his tenants, two villeins (villagers) and three bordars (smallholders) also had two ploughs between them, each plough representing eight oxen. In 1086 Rotherwas had a value of £6.

Around the middle of the 15th century the estate became the principal seat of the Bodenham family and would remain so for the next 460 years. Many of the rooms were lavishly decorated, the walls being covered in panelling of oak, yew, acacia and sycamore. King James I visited Rotherwas on at least two occasions and even had his own set of rooms put aside for him. His courtiers were so delighted with the place that they wanted to stay there beyond their planned time. This prompted James to remark, *'Non datur cuivis adire*

Rotherwas' – 'Everyone may not live at Rotherwas', a remark that was passed down as a local proverb.

During the Civil War a Scottish army under Lord Leven that was besieging Royalist Hereford in 1645 sent two bailiffs and four musketeers to Rotherwas to plunder anything of value. Buildings became derelict and the chapel was unused for over 20 years as the family struggled to pay a number of fines over the course of the conflict.

In 1675 Thomas Blount, a 17th-century historian, described the house as follows:

> This is a delicious seat, situate near the river Wye and within two myles of Hereford, abounding with store of excellent fruit rich meadows, and fertile arable; having also a Park within less than half a myle of the house where there is a neat lodge upon a hill that overlooks the whole country adjacent. ... The house is partly of old timber work, but one end of it was new built of stone in the last age by Sir Roger, where there is a fayre parlour full of coats of arms according to that age; and over that a noble dyning room, wainscoted with walnut tree, and on the mantel-tree of the chimney twenty five coats of arms in one achievement with this motto:- VERITAS LIBERABIT. There is also a fayre gate-house of brick and near that the Chapel, now disused, an abundance of out-houses, all mortgaged and gong to ruyne through the misfortunes of the Family.

It was not until the 1700s that the Bodenham family regained their wealth and in 1731 they built a new 11-bay mansion on a nearby site to the designs of James Gibbs. The house contained a 28-foot long dining room, a library/billiard room and a 36-foot long conservatory. Upstairs were located 11 principal rooms, five dressing rooms, nine servants' bedrooms, linen rooms, box rooms and domestic offices. Much of the Jacobean panelling and several of the stone fireplaces were taken from the old house and installed in the new residence. The new house was built of bricks that were transported up the River Wye following the establishment of the newly formed Wye Navigation Company on the Board of which the Bodenham family had seats. A wharf was constructed on the banks of the river and the Woolhope Club

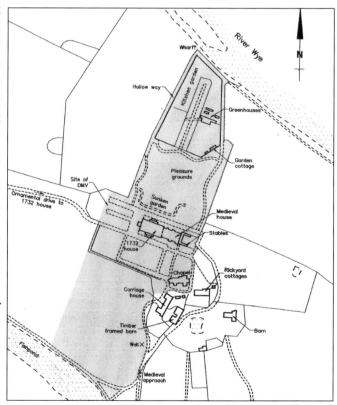

Plan of showing Rotherwas House and its surroundings, part of the green area being that now scheduled as a grade 2 listed site

mention a trip they made in 1890 around the Rotherwas Estate where they were shown a '... fine oak on the river bank, below the garden, to one of whose enormous boughs were formally attached the scales for weighing coals etc. when landed from the barges thirty years previously'.

1904 Ordnance Survey map showing the parkland around the house. It also shows the line taken by the railway and below it 'the straight mile', referred to in other chapters

A deer park is shown around the house on the county maps of Bowen in 1762 and Taylor in 1786, and the park is also shown on an illustration of the house made in 1790. When the new house was built, however, the deer park was reduced to an area adjacent to the house (as shown on the 1832 OS 1" map) and new pleasure grounds were created. New formal gardens were laid out which featured a sunken lawn with shrubberies to either side, together with a walled garden. The latter had a greenhouse, forcing houses and a gardener's cottage. Also included was a tree-lined walk down to the river comprised of pairs of Irish Junipers, trees that stand to this day.

Alongside the new house was Rotherwas Chapel. The earliest part of the chapel is the nave, which was probably built in the 14th century. A fireplace situated high up the north wall was presumably associated with a gallery used by the family. The chapel was largely rebuilt in the 16th century when the present roof, dated to 1589, was added. The tower was added around 1730 and once held a clock made by Thomas Hildeyard, who was a priest at the chapel and a noted amateur clockmaker. At one time the hour hand was removed because of a ghost that allegedly appeared every time the clock showed 1am. The clock was subsequently sold to be replaced by a Victorian one. Further work was carried out in 1884 by the Countess Irena de la Barre Bodenham and Peter Paul Pugin, youngest son of Augustus Welby Pugin. This included the construction of the south chantry chapel, sanctuary and sacristy, the rebuilding of the south porch as a small chapel and the creation of a new entry through the tower. The chapel was beautifully decorated and has several fine stained glass windows.

Rotherwas House as sketched by James Wathen in 1799

Rotherwas House in the early 1900s

Charles Thomas Bodenham inherited the house in the late 19th century and entered into many local business arrangements, including being an appointed proprietor of The Horse Towing Path Company and part owner of The City and County Bank. The bank got into financial difficulties during the 1825 banking crisis and in order to save the bank Charles mortgaged the estate, a burden from which it never fully recovered. Throughout the 19th century efforts were made to put the estate back on a secure financial footing but all to no avail. After Charles' death the estate and its debts passed to his son, Charles de la Barre Bodenham. Charles and his wife, Irena Maria, the daughter of Count Dzierzykras Morawski, had no children. Following the sudden death of Charles at the Hotel Wagram in Paris his wife inherited the estate.

During the period of time between her husband's death and her own, Irena had the St Charles home in Lower Bullingham built for the retired and poor of the estate. Previously the family had also been responsible for the construction of two convents in the neighbouring village of Bullingham. The Sisters of Charity at St Elizabeth's was an active order with schools and other ventures, whereas The Poor Clares at St Raphael's was a contemplative order.

Following Irena's death the estate passed into the hands of her cousin Count Louis Pomain Bodenham Lubienski. The Count married Evelyn Stratford, the daughter of John Stratford of the clan of Kirwan of Moyne, County Galway, Ireland. They had three sons.

Count Louis Pomain Bodenham Lubienski and his wife Evelyn with one of their sons

Mr Jenkins, the coachman at Rotherwas House c.*1900*

The Rotherwas Estate Football Team c.1900. Mr Jenkins, the coachman, stands at the back

The family chose not to live at Rotherwas but settled at Bullingham Manor, renting out Rotherwas House to a Mr Robert Mackworth-Praed.

In January 1907 a serious fire broke out in the stables and was in danger of spreading to the main house. In a 'Flashback' article in the *Hereford Times* for 19th October 1995, Nigel Heins recounted how the then head of Hereford's police and fire brigade, Frank Richardson, was faced with a dilemma:

Two of the county's most precious buildings were at risk as flames raged nearby, but the rules stated that he should ignore the blaze!

Fire had broken out in the stables and coachhouse at the Rotherwas estate. It was sad news because the fine, three-storey building, although put to humble use, was said to resemble a gentleman's country residence. But a far greater tragedy threatened because the flames menaced Rotherwas House itself and the historic Rotherwas Chapel. News of impending disaster was carried to Hereford by Rotherwas coachman John Ayriss who entreated the city brigade to save the architectural masterpiece.

Only days earlier, after a debate with the rural district council, Hereford Town Council ruled that its firemen should not tackle any conflagrations outside the city boundary.

What a quandry faced Richardson that day in 1907! The thoughts of flames dealing out damage without opposition wounded his professional pride and he set about seeking a change of heart from his bosses.

As the blaze ripped through the stable block from corner to corner Richardson realised words had to come before water if he was to save mansion and chapel. He jumped into Ayriss's carriage and pair and raced to see the Mayor George Jackson Caldwell and the deputy Edwyn Gurney. There was deep consternation over a request to overturn such a recently passed rule and the civic heads consulted a third councillor, Alderman Witts. The trio decreed heritage was more important than the minute book and gave the chief firefighter the go-ahead to rush to Rotherwas.

Within seconds the fire station was alive with men who had been summoned by electric bells. Six horses were called up from the Green Dragon Posting Co and four of them were harnessed to the steam engine *Nell Gwynne*. With a man riding postillion on one of the leaders 'she' was soon hurtling towards the scene. Following a few minutes later was the city manual [fire engine] drawn by a pair of horses.

Pictures of the fire-damaged coachhouse and stables

HEREFORDSHIRE.

About 2 miles from the ancient Cathedral City of Hereford, which is well served by the Great Western, the London and North Western and the Midland Railway Companies.

Edwards, Russell & Baldwin

Are instructed by the Trustees of the late COUNT BODENHAM-LUBIENSKI, to offer for Sale by Auction,

At the GREEN DRAGON HOTEL, HEREFORD,

On Thursday, the 5th day of September, 1912,

AT 11.30 A.M. PUNCTUALLY, THE

Exceedingly Attractive Freehold Residential & Sporting Property,

KNOWN AS THE

ROTHERWAS ESTATE

COMPRISING AN

EXCELLENT FAMILY MANSION,

DISTINGUISHED AS

ROTHERWAS HOUSE,

Approached by a carriage drive with Lodge Entrance, and standing in picturesque grounds bounded by the River Wye, which provides about

FOUR MILES OF FIRST-RATE SALMON FISHING,

The *River Wye* being well-known as one of the best *Salmon Rivers* in England.

There is ample Stabling (recently rebuilt), also Productive Fruit and Vegetable Gardens. The Property, which extends over an area of about

2,578 ACRES,

ALSO INCLUDES A NUMBER OF

VALUABLE FARMS & SMALL HOLDINGS

(renowned for the great fertility of the soil, which is undoubtedly some of the richest in the highly-cultivated County of Hereford),

WOODS & COTTAGES,

the whole producing an actual and estimated Rental of

£4,655 PER ANNUM.

The Estate will be offered first as a whole, and if not sold, then in numerous convenient Lots, unless an acceptable offer be previously made by private treaty

Copies of these Particulars may be had of Messrs. WITHAM, ROSKELL, MUNSTER & WELD, Solicitors, 1 Gray's Inn Square, London; Mr. HENRY H. CAVE, Estate Office, Rugby; or of the AUCTIONEERS,

Leominster, Hereford, and Tenbury.

According to the *Hereford Times* it was not long before two jets of water were playing on the burning mass which was surrounded by a huge crowd of people drawn from all parts of the district 'on foot, a-wheel, and by trap, countless cyclists from Hereford having followed in the wake of the engines ...'.

The Count died in 1909 and the trustees, owing to mounting debts, decided to put the whole estate of 2,500 acres on the market. In 1912 a catalogue was produced which listed the sale of Rotherwas House plus 15 farms, 19 smallholdings, 25 cottages and a blacksmith's shop together with shooting and fishing rights. Several lots were sold but many were not. The contents of the house were also sold and most were purchased by the antique dealers Charles of London. They sold on the wall panelling to America where it now forms part of the Rotherwas Room in Amherst College, Massachusetts.

Some of the panelling at Rotherwas House that was put up for auction in 1912

Top left: Early 17th-century oak panelling and mantel in the Julius Caesar room. This was reused from the earlier house

Top right: Early 17th-century walnut panelling in the banqueting hall, again reused from the earlier house

Left: Oak chimney piece in the largely walnut banqueting hall. The shield contains the 25 quarterings of the Bodenhams

TELEPHONE No.
1938 REGENT.

OSBORN & MERCER.

TELEGRAPHIC ADDRESS:
"OVERBID, PICCY, LONDON."

"ROTHERWAS"
TWO-AND-A-HALF MILES FROM HEREFORD.

BY Messrs. OSBORN & MERCER.

IMPORTANT SALE BY AUCTION
OF THE

VALUABLE ANTIQUE FURNITURE

Including many fine examples of

CHIPPENDALE, SHERATON, ADAM, ETC.

EARLY ENGLISH MIRRORS AND CLOCKS. Valuable
SPECIMEN BORDERED TAPESTRY PANEL, ETC.

ALSO THE

RARE OLD PANELLINGS AND CARVINGS

with the Mantelpieces, Overmantels, and Doors to the principal
rooms, in Walnut, Oak, and other woods

On the 11th MARCH, 1913, and three following days, on the premises.

May be viewed by Card, privately, on Friday and Saturday, 7th and
8th March, and publicly on Monday, 10th March. — Illustrated
Catalogues (1s. each), may be obtained of Messrs. LAMBE,
CARLESS & SON, Solicitors, Hereford; or of the Auctioneers, at
their Offices, 28B, Albemarle Street, Piccadilly, W.

AT A LOW UP-SET PRICE.

MESSRS. OSBORN & MERCER have also been instructed to offer the Mansion House, "ROTHERWAS," above referred to, for SALE BY AUCTION, at the conclusion
of the Sale of Furniture, on the 14th of March next. The Mansion is well adapted for conversion into an

INSTITUTION, COLLEGE, OR RESIDENTIAL HOTEL.

as there is very extensive accommodation, and the gardens and grounds are delightfully matured and attractive. A special feature is the well-grown Yew hedges. Included in the
Sale will be the right of fishing along

ONE-AND-A-HALF MILES OF THE RIVER WYE.

The total area is about 10 ACRES.—Particulars, with plan and conditions of Sale, may be obtained from Messrs. LAMBE, CARLESS & SON, Solicitors, Hereford, or of the
Auctioneers, at their Offices.

"ALBEMARLE HOUSE," 28b, ALBEMARLE STREET, PICCADILLY, W.

A 360 degree view of the Rotherwas Room in Amherst College showing the panelling that came from Rotherwas House

The house was later commandeered by the Ministry of Defence to house the soldiers who guarded the Rotherwas Munitions Factory during the Great War. After the war was over the house, near enough derelict, was sold off as a source of building materials. The size of the mansion can be gauged by the quantity of items listed: 200,000 square feet of timber, 400,000 dressed bricks, 20,000 roofing tiles, 10,000 roofing slates, 115 pine & oak doors, 100 glazed sashes, 10,000 square feet of stone flagged paving and a large quantity of old oak beams and joists. So ended the existence of a fine Herefordshire mansion. The last service to be held in the chapel was in 1914. Having been stripped of most of its fixtures and fittings, it was used as a potato store and even for rearing pigs. Thankfully English Heritage took over the chapel in August 1961 and restored it, bringing in artefacts and furnishing from other places of worship in their care.

The *Hereford Times* of January 1913 contains an article on the fate of Rotherwas Chapel in what is probably the most evocative piece of journalism I have ever read concerning the estate:

THE FATE OF ROTHERWAS

39 BODIES REMOVED FROM THE CHAPEL

STRANGE PROCEEDINGS

It would be difficult indeed to find in Herefordshire history parallel to the strange work now going on in the ancient private chapel at Rotherwas, near Hereford – a direct result of the recent sale of the Rotherwas estate, of which the little sanctuary has been a venerated feature for over three centuries. The three or four Hereford men employed there in what seems nothing more or less than licenced sacrilege are literally living amongst the dead, and will be glad when their unpleasant task is completed. The bodies being thus rudely, albeit reverentially, disturbed are mainly those of the Bodenham family, whose long reign at Rotherwas has just concluded. With the permission of the new owner of the building and the sanction of the Home Office, the remains are being exhumed for reinterment in the little cemetery hard by on the same estate, where lie the late Count Louis Bodenham Lubienski and his wife, and also other members of the Roman Catholic community centred at Lower Bullingham, less than a mile distant. A faculty from the Home Secretary was obtained by Mr H.H. Cave, of Rugby, the estate agent, who is acting on behalf of the surviving members of the family, the late Count Bodenham Lubienski, who for some years lived at Bullingham Manor, having left three sons, all of whom are still minors.

SEVENTEENTH CENTURY INTERMENTS

One of the earliest interments known to have taken place in the chapel dates from June, 1691, and possibly there were some before this, as the building was erected, it was believed, in 1583; and in view of these facts it was only after much deliberation that the drastic course of exhumation was decided upon, in the belief that it is the intention of the new owner, a gentleman well known in business circles in Hereford, to demolish the chapel. It is, of course, to prevent any possible desecration of the graves of the household in future that the bodies are being removed to another resting place. It was indeed a strange experience that a representative of the Hereford Times who visited the scene had on Wednesday. What is transpiring would, he says, greatly distress the sensitive mind which regards the burial-place of a human being as a hallowed spot, and when that burial-place lies within the walls of a building devoted for centuries to the worship of God, to disturb it seems nothing less than sacrilege. The little chapel is now a veritable charnel house – an apartment for dry bones. The stone floor is up, and just in front of the altar is a deep excavation; one of many that has yielded up long-buried secrets. Close by is a large oak coffin which the breast plate tells us contains the mortal remains of Irena Maria de la Barre Bodenham, who was born July 26th, 1822, and died December 10th, 1892. She was evidently the last person to be buried in the church. In the tiny side chapel, with its stained glass window, is the open vault from which the coffin has been raised, and at the time of writing it still contained the remains of Charles de le Barre Bodenham, who passed away in 1883. To add to the gruesomeness of the situation this coffin is covered with water. Over it is a pulley suspended on rough timber-work, which accords ill with the sacred surroundings.

Two men were engaged in pulling down the altar, and a third was removing a modern iron safe let into the wall of the east end. Turning round, a glance towards the west end revealed a pile of stout new wooden boxes, the majority of them of uniform size, looking very much like superior currant boxes in a grocer's warehouse. These all contain the few remaining bones – all reverentially collected – of Bodenhams who 'had their day then ceased to be' long ago. In accordance with the instructions of the Home Secretary, all these boxes have been well pitched inside and covered with charcoal dust, which has antiseptic qualities. In the majority of the cases not a vestige of the original coffin remains, but some of the bodies are enclosed in leaden caskets still in a good state of preservation, and for reinterment these are also being placed in new wooden cases.

REMAINS IDENTIFIED

Amongst the remains that have been discovered and identified by the breast plates or records of the church are the following:-

Maria Bodenham, June 7th 1691.
Fanny Bodenham, November 3rd 1706.
Jacet Johannes Bodenham, October 24th 1718.

Inside Rotherwas Chapel in 2009
(© Logaston Press)

Rotherwas Chapel in 2014

Anna Bodenham, September 9th 1736.
Rogerus Bodenham, September 13th 1739.
Thomas Hiltleyard, March 30th 1746.
Anna Bodenham, 1754.
Hilda Hester (surname indecipherable), December 10th 1756.
Carolo Thomae de Bodenham, December 5th 1760.
Jacet Carolus Bodenham, 1762.
Charles Stonor Bodenham, April 10th 1764.
Francis Bodenham, March 25th 1803.
Bridget Mary Bodenham, April 29th 1805.
J.C. Corby, June 22nd 1815.
Charles Bodenham, April 5th 1826.
Elizabeth Marie Weld de Lylworth, March 3rd 1807.
Phillip Fielding, December 7th 1877.
Charles de la Barre Bodenham, June 21st 1883.
Irena de la Barre Bodenham, December 10th 1892.

Outside the church, on the south side, the remains of a little girl named Minnie West, age 6, have been dug up. She was buried, it was said, about 30 years ago. The skull is well preserved, and when discovered was filled with soil, in which tender tree roots were growing! The skull of a woman found inside the church displayed a perfect set of teeth, in which there is no sign of decay, though they had been buried 80 years. Altogether 39 bodies have been discovered. By order of the Home Secretary the reinterment is to take place as quietly as possible, and the religious ceremony will, we understand, be conducted by the Prior of Belmont Pro-Cathedral.

ROTHERWAS HISTORY

Rotherwas is said to be one of the oldest Roman Catholic estates in the Country, but the chapel, it is believed, was originally erected as a Protestant church by the Bodenham of the period, who, having become a Protestant, recanted shortly prior to his death and returned to the Roman Catholic faith. It is a point of controversy whether the chapel is Protestant or Roman Catholic. There is no record of its having been consecrated and its history appears to be mainly tradition.

The men and women whose bones are now being unearthed, in their day and generation created a family history that occupies a conspicuous place in the annals of the county. The name of George Bodenham first appears in the reign of Henry I; and in that of Edward I we find William Bodenham, a descendant. It was through a marriage with Isabella, daughter and heiress of Walter de la Barre, that the family obtained the

Aerial photograph showing the site of Rotherwas House. The outlines of the house and gardens can be clearly seen as parchmarks in the grass in the centre of the picture. The chapel is towards the top left amongst the trees, with the coachhouse just above it. Near the bottom left is Garden Cottage and the remains of the sunken pleasure garden. The edge of Hereford's sewage works can be seen in the bottom right-hand corner.
(© Herefordshire Council)

largest acquisition of property. Walter de la Barre, of Barns Court in this county, left an only daughter, who became the second wife of Roger Bodenham, and brought with her several great estates in the parishes of Dewchurch, Kilpeck, etc. Rotherwas, which is supposed to have derived its name from a parish in the Hundred of Broxash, also formed part of the property of the de la Barres and came to the family by this marriage. The first of the family who lived at Rotherwas was Roger Bodenham, who married Joan Brownich in the 15th century, and the last Count Bodenham Lubienski, who died in 1909. ... In the civil wars the Bodenham family suffered severely through their loyalty to the Roman Catholic faith, many of their estates being confiscated.

This fine old Herefordshire family Rotherwas will know no more, and the name of Bodenham, which has stood for so long for all that is best in country life, now disappears from the county. The estate has been disposed of to many different purchasers, and in all probability a hundred and eighty-five acres surrounding the mansion will be split up into smallholdings, the County Council having agreed to buy this portion subject to the sanctions of the Board of Agriculture being obtained. Mr Mackworth Praed, the last occupant, quitted the mansion in June of last year, to the great regret of the whole neighbourhood, and the house is still vacant. The coming change appears to be regarded with some apprehension by some people and one of Mr Praed's old employees remarked to a Hereford Times reporter this week; 'one gentleman like Mr Mackworth Praed will do the county more good than 50 smallholders. I have lost the best of masters.'

The remains of a pair of semi-detached estate cottages that stand several hundred yards to the east of the site of Rotherwas House

5   Rotherwas's Overgrown Graves

by Chris Over

There are four memorial stones hidden away in undergrowth several hundred yards south of Rotherwas Chapel. It is believed that these were moved to this spot when it was announced that Rotherwas Chapel was to be demolished. The chapel was reprieved and the demolition never took place but the news came too late for the memorials which had already been relocated. Sometime later several of the Bodenham family bodies were removed and repatriated to their homeland of Poland, leaving behind the four shown below. Amongst those removed was Count Louis Bodenham Lubienski, but the remains of his wife remained in situ.

Of your charity pray for the repose of the souls of
John Stratford Kirwan born September 21st 1836 deceased November 20th 1892
of his beloved wife Victoria Mary Louisa daughter of George, Marquis of Hastings
born July 18th 1837 deceased March 30th 1888
of Sybil Flora their daughter born May 22nd 1863 deceased July 18th 1886.
and of George Augustus Reginald their youngest son born May 11th 1871
Deceased April 18th 1892.

Sweet Jesus
grant eternal rest to the soul of
EVELYN
beloved wife of Count Louis Bodenham Lubienski
born 15th October 1861. Married 27th November 1895.
Died 6th March 1902

In loving memory of Samuel Gregory
who died July 17th 1902, aged 58 years

Above is a funeral card for Samuel Gregory; these
were widely used in the late 1800s and early 1900s.

John Reidy
died August 3rd 1903, aged 58 years

6   St Andrew's Church, Dinedor

by Peter Houghton

The correct ecclesiastical name of the parish is Dyndor and the parish church is listed as St Andrew's, Dyndor. However, in this chapter, except for quotations, 'Dinedor' is used for both village and parish.

The ecclesiastical parish includes the part of Dinedor containing the church, as well as houses on all sides of Dinedor Hill, and extends down to the River Wye to include the eastern half of the Rotherwas industrial estate, Sink Green Farm and Dinedor Court. Although formerly the parish included land on the other side of the River Wye near Hampton Bishop, this was transferred to Hampton Bishop parish in 1884.[1] The church at Holme Lacy was closed in 1992 and the parish of Dinedor with Holme Lacy was formed in 1994 by amalgamating the two parishes, so the current ecclesiastical parish is fairly extensive, reaching as far south as Bolstone Wood.

St Andrew's Church (© Derek Foxton Archives)

The parish church of St Andrew's lies between Glebe Farm and a field known as The Garrison or Garrison Meadow, to the south-east of the village. 'Glebe' means land belonging to the church so, in former days, the rent for the land would be paid by the farmer to the Rector of the church. Somewhat unusually it is approached by a path over private land belonging to Glebe Farm, alongside a small stream. Since the modern village consists of several scattered collections of houses, there is no real village centre, meaning the church fulfils that role to some extent. The south and west of the church look across the 'Garrison' field to Aconbury Hill.

Although Christians are likely to have worshipped together in Dinedor for many years before the 13th century, the first mention of a church dates from that century and it is thought likely that a church was built during the reign of Henry III (1217-72) and who, famed for his piety, built many churches throughout England.[2]

The earliest illustrations of the original church date from the first half of the 19th century, notably a watercolour by C.F. Walker as one of a pair in a frame hung on the north wall of the nave. The two pictures are of Dinedor Church, dated 1850, and of Holme Lacy Church dated 1857. Dinedor Church looks similar in appearance to the present building but it was in 1867, not long after the painting was made, that its condition was deemed to be so bad that rebuilding was the only option. It 'had fallen into such decay and was so dilapidated, that the only wonder is how it had held together at all. Besides its insecurity it was dark, damp and incommodius.'[3]

The church was rebuilt 1867-68 by F.R. Kempson in the Early English style, with a simple nave and chancel and a small tower surmounted by a pyramidal roof, thus resembling the former church in appearance, though larger. The tower was retained from the old building but all the rest was rebuilt, much of the original building material being recycled and used in the new church. The exterior of the present building is of coursed local sandstone with Bath stone dressing, while the interior is of ashlar stone obtained locally from Ballingham.[4] Not all the original material was recycled; the remains of what is thought to be a Norman window were recently unearthed in the graveyard by excavations under the auspices of the Dinedor Heritage Group.[5]

The foundation stone of the new building was laid in mid-June 1867 on a 'day brilliant with sunshine' and a sermon given by the archdeacon Lord Saye and Sele concluded with the words 'Let us heartily pray that as in the ancient church, so hereafter in the new building the Word of God preached within the walls may be delivered with truth, zeal and efficacy'.[6] Apparently the churchyard at the time was full of the remains of the old building as well as two chests, one of wood and one of iron. The chests are not mentioned in subsequent accounts so apparently were destroyed or sold.

The new church was opened 12 months later in June 1868 and again the weather was good. The prayers and lessons were read by the Rector, Revd Rowland Muckleston, while the Provost of Worcester College Oxford, the patron of the living, preached the sermon.

The new church cost £700.[7] A sign in the present vestry states that 'The Incorporated Society for Building and Churches granted £30 in 1866 towards rebuilding the church with additional accommodation for 26 persons, the entire area to accommodate 91 at least, the sittings are all free and subject to allotment by the churchwardens, suitable provision being made for poorer inhabitants.'

The church, unlike the comparatively new rectory, survived what became known as the Hereford Earthquake of 1896 unscathed.[8] The Revd Muckleston compiled the following report on the damage the earthquake caused to the Rectory: 'There were two sets of vibrations at 5.30 in the morning. The second, following five or six seconds after the first, was the weaker of the two. Every room in the house was filled with soot, mortar and broken stones. This arose from the ruin of the chimneys, eight in number. These were knocked down and all had to be rebuilt. If there was any rumbling it was drowned by the crash of the fallen chimneys.'

Some renovations to the church tower were carried out in 1987 assisted by a substantial financial contribution by Miss Helen Preece, according to a framed notice on the interior wall of the tower near the font. Helen Preece lived in Melbourne, Australia and her connection with Dinedor was that her paternal grandmother was interred in the churchyard, having died on 20th March 1950 aged 80.

The church interior and furnishings

The chancel

The church has two stained glass windows. The older and larger one is the East Window in the chancel, which is a triptych portraying Christ as the Good Shepherd in the centre flanked on the left by St John and on the right by St Andrew, the patron saint of the church. The east window was donated in 1899 by Revd E.C. Adams, Rector 1897-1904 and was made by Jones and Willis.[9] The other stained glass window is found in the south wall of the nave and is inscribed 'In proud and loving memory of the Dinedor boys who fell in the Great War 1914-19'. ('Boys' ignores Mary Morton, a nurse who served in a Serbian field hospital, who is at least remembered in the Roll of Service memorial nearby!) The window is of two separate lights, depicting Valour and Fortitude on the left and right respectively, and the influence of Art Nouveau can be discerned in the design. The window was designed by J.H. Dearle, made by Morris and Co. and installed in 1921.[10]

The altar frontal was originally embroidered in Victorian times and was restored by the Hereford Cathedral Broderers as a Millennium Project. The renewed frontal was dedicated in 2000 by the Bishop of Ludlow. Its centrepiece is a depiction of the Lamb of God, a common Biblical title of Jesus,[11] carrying a St George's flag pennant, while the two side pieces are worked designs of Alpha and Omega, used figuratively in Greek for 'Beginning and End', referring to God (see photograph overleaf).[12]

The south wall of the chancel has a commemorative brass plate for Revd Muckleston (see below under 'Incumbents').

The two chairs in the chancel were carved by John Gaines in 1901. Gaines was carpenter for the Rotherwas estate for many years and Clerk to the Parish. He also carved two candlesticks and a cross from pieces of a yew tree in the churchyard. These are still used on the altar for public worship. Graves of several members of the Gaines family lie in the churchyard near the north-west corner of the church (see also chapter 20).

The incumbent's stall is fairly recent and has a small brass plaque saying 'In memoriam TEB JEB 1929', but the identity of these two people has not been found.

The altar frontal in St Andrew's Church

The nave

The nave contains pews made from pine and although electric lighting is now used, Victorian brass oil lamps marked 'Millers Vestal – made in USA' remain on the walls.

On the south wall of the nave, flanking the window of remembrance, are memorials to people from the village who served in the First World War. On the left-hand side facing the window is a brass Roll of Service with 28 names, while on the right-hand side is a framed Roll of Honour with 40 names. Presumably the brass plate commemorates those who lost their lives. If so, this would be a 70% death rate, and is a sobering reminder of the devastating effect of the war on the population of young men in every community in the UK at the time. Above the brass Roll of Service, there is a small brass plate with five names, inscribed 'Roll of Honour'. Presumably these are the names of those who were killed in the Second World War, but this is not explicit. Two of the names are the same as those in the larger plate so it is likely that they were related, most likely father and son. Both the 1914-19 Roll of Honour and the Roll of Service are a little unusual because they contain the name of a woman, Mary Morton. According to the Roll of Honour, she was a nurse in a Serbian relief hospital. The Roll of Service gives details of where all those listed served and it is of interest that three men were stokers on the same warship, *HMS Gorgon*.

The brass memorial to Bertie Davies (see below under **Churchyard**) is also on the south wall of the nave.

The west wall of the nave has an arch which gives access to the bottom floor of the bell tower. Above the arch is a royal coat of arms of George III, painted in oil and dating from 1820. On the flanking walls are painted wooden panels, that on the left listing the Ten

Looking west down the nave to the entrance to the belltower

Commandments, and that on the right detailing the donations made in the time of Revd Charles Bird (see below).

The north wall of the nave has the framed watercolour of the church dated 1850 (see above). There is also a brass plaque, donated 'by the teachers of Herefordshire as a token of their esteem' commemorating the career of Anne Amry Andrew who was headmistress of the village school 1892-1909.

In the north-east corner of the nave is a wooden pulpit with a small plaque noting that it was erected in memory of Revd D'Arcy S. Morton, who was Rector 1914-27.

Along the altar rail are kneelers attractively worked in dark blue with contrasting yellow and white lettering and design. These were made over several years in the 1980s by members of the congregation, chiefly Jean Savage and Margaret Hornsby.[13]

The belltower

The belltower contains three bells, hung in a mediaeval frame made in about 1400. This frame is fragile so the bells are not rung frequently these days and when they are, caution is taken. The oldest bell is the smallest and was cast by John Pennington II of Monmouth in 1675. The other two bells are much more recent, having been cast in 1899 and 1923 respectively, the latter one as a war memorial. These two bells replace bells cast in 1675 and 1694.[14]

The floor of the belltower contains the font, an octagonal design made of limestone and dating from the 15th century, although the font cover is modern. Marshall describes the font as 'very perfect and a graceful example of an octagonal font'.[15]

On the north and south sides of the belltower are marble monuments to Revd Charles Bird (see below under **Incumbents**) and various members of the Allen family. The oldest plaque commemorates Revd Edward Allen, who died on 20th December 1805. Presumably related to Edward was Henry Allen, who is remembered by a monument as dying on 28th August 1829 aged 65, and is named as 'the second son of Rev William Allen'. There are also memorials to Henry Allen's daughter, Catherine, who died on 15th February 1863 aged 68, and to his widow, also called Catherine, who died aged 76 in 1842. The memorial mentions that his widow was the daughter of the late William Bird, so presumably she was related (sister?) to the Rector at the time, Revd Charles Bird.

The other monuments in the belltower are to Francis Brickenden (see **Incumbents** below), his wife Anne (who died on 24th December 1823 aged 86) and their eldest daughter Anne, who was only 13 when she died on 4th June 1782.

As well as displays of photographs of the local insects and wild flowers likely to be found in the churchyard, the belltower also has two books of colour photographs portraying two exhibitions held at the church, a craft exhibition held on 9th and 10th June 1990 and a Festival of Memories held in 2008 (see **The church as a community in recent years** below).

Fairly high on the wall of the west end of the belltower is the carved wooden reredos which, until about 1975 was behind the altar. It is dated 1898 and is thought to have been carved by John Gaines, who was the carpenter on the Rotherwas estate.[16]

The vestry

The vestry does not have a door separating it from the chancel but the organ forms some sort of partition. The present organ is electronic, as was the previous one, and was acquired in early 2014, having previously been used at St Francis' church on the South Wye estate. In the vestry hang wooden plaques giving details of the benefaction from the Incorporated Society for Building and Churches for rebuilding the church and of Revd Charles Bird's investment to support the school.

The plate used for celebrating Holy Communion consists of silver chalice, paten and salver and dates from the early 18th century. The salver is engraved 'Dedit Carolus: Johannes Bird [Charles John Bird] a.m. and S.A.S. Rector Dynedor. Gloria Deo soli 1836'. The back of the salver is hallmarked 1717 and engraved with the motto of Charles Bird 'Cruce Spes Mea' ('My hope is the cross').

The paten for the chalice originates from the same time and is engraved 'RT Parochice Rector Hoc operculum dono dedit Dynder 1717'. 'RT' refers to Richard Traherne, who was Rector 1692-1731, and the inscription says that he gave the paten to the church. It was made by a Richard Bayley.

The chalice itself is not hallmarked but is mentioned in a list of plate from about 1830.[17]

The churchyard

The churchyard is rectangular and bounded by a stone wall. There are three gates, one in the west wall giving access to the porch from the path from the road, one to the south-east leading on to Garrison Meadow, and one on the north-west corner leading to the Rectory. This path is now over private land and is not a right of way.

*Revd A.S. Walpole laying a memorial stone
in the wall around the extension to the graveyard in 1906*

The churchyard is still in use as a burial ground. It was extended in 1906 southwards and a memorial stone was laid on 16th August 1906 by Revd A.S. Walpole, Rector at that time, in the new wall, as is shown in the photograph above. It has recently been found lying in the field, presumably having been displaced at some stage.

Most of the tombstones are made of local sandstone and the older ones have weathered badly so that inscriptions have been lost or have become illegible. The oldest legible gravestone has been moved from its original position and now stands against the north wall of the church. The stone commemorates Mathias Turner and his wife Theodosia who died in 1659 and 1690 respectively. Mathias was the vicar of 'Hom Lacie and Parson of Dineder'.

Also along the north wall of the church, near the porch, is a small railed enclosure with the pink granite tomb of Revd Rowland Muckleston (see below under **Incumbents**) who died in 1897.

Most of the gravestones record simply the death and age of the person interred, together with expressions of love and Christian hope, but two graves are somewhat unusual. The first grave of note is that of Edwin Thomas Bray of Cooks Yard Farm, Abbey Dore, who died aged 42 on 2nd October 1878 after falling out of a dog cart. The other has a granite cross which marks the grave of Albert Ernest ('Bertie') Davies, aged 16, who died on 8th June 1906 after saving two of his friends from drowning in the River Wye and attempting to save a third. His self-sacrifice was praised and recorded by the Royal Humane Society as an illuminated address, the vote for this to be done having been passed unanimously at its meeting on 15th October 1906. The funeral for Bertie was conducted by the Bishop of Hereford on 14th July and a full account of the service is given in an account by William Mason, written in 1907 and presented to 7,000 schoolchildren in Herefordshire who contributed to the cost of the marble slab and cross on the grave.

Mason wrote the following poem for Bertie's parents:

O sweet be thy sleep in the garden of flowers
Resting awhile from the heat of the day,
The requiem song in the long silent hours,
The moaning of dove and the wild cushat's [wood pigeon] lay.

Thy voice was the song of the lark in the morning,
As it rose up to God, through the ether of blue;
The dawn of thy manhood the village adorning
Thou brave noble soul, so loving and true.

O can there be light in the dark vale of sorrow?
O pity the home, see the one vacant chair;
God grant to their hearts sweet solace to borrow
For the one that is absent, though constantly there.

Let Thine own healing balm drop down in their sleeping,
Oblivion shut out the cold dews from their bed,
Triumphant the song after sorrow and weeping,
The hero still lives, though we mourn him as dead.

The granite cross that marks the grave of Albert Ernest ('Bertie') Davies

There is also a brass memorial to Bertie inside the church on the south wall of the nave.

Miss Christine Evans, the daughter of the Rector from 1932-1942, who was inspired to found the Dinedor Sports Day, is buried in an unmarked grave near the wall close to the northwest corner of the church.[18]

Near this grave is a seat which was donated in memory of Stephen Charles Payne who was killed by an avalanche in Snowdonia on 28th January 1986 aged 22.[19]

The churchyard contains a variety of wildflowers including drifts of snowdrops and daffodils, so is particularly attractive in the Spring. It contains six yew trees, with a seventh tree just outside the wall by the path leading to the old rectory to the left of the gate giving access to the church porch. These trees are fairly large and probably over 200 years old.[20] Snowdrops, because of their symbolic purity of whiteness, were formerly used to decorate churches for the festival of the Purification of the Virgin Mary on 2nd February, otherwise known as the feast of the Presentation in the Temple or Candlemas.[21]

The Rectory

Prior to 1855, no Rectory existed in Dinedor, the Rector being based at Mordiford. No written record could be found of where curates were housed, although oral tradition says that they were accommodated at Glebe Farm.[22] In 1855 a Rectory was built for Dinedor about 250 metres from the church and connected with the church, via the old school house, by a footpath. The footpath does not appear to have been a Right of Way since it now goes through private land and a notice near the church gate nearest the porch forbids public access.

The Rectory is an attractive building with stone gables and was designed by T. Nicholson.[23] It is now a private dwelling called Dinedor Hall, having ceased being a Rectory at least as long ago as 1959 when it was sold to a Mrs Clifton.[24] The vicarage at Holme Lacy became the residence of the Rector, and then of the team member responsible for some of the rural parishes[25] until Holme Lacy church was closed in 1992.

Incumbents

Worcester College, Oxford University, has been the patron of the living of Dinedor since 1855, when Revd Rowland Muckleston, who had been Vice-Provost of the college, became Rector.[26] However, there is a memorial in the bell tower to a Revd Edward Allen, who died in 1805 and was a Fellow of Worcester College, so the connections between the College and the church appear to go back further than 1855. (The position of Revd Edward Allen regarding the church is not clear. He is not listed as Rector. Since he was only 37 at death it is unlikely that he had retired from a living elsewhere.) The link has continued until the present and the Team Rector is still occasionally invited to preach at Worcester College. A chronological list of incumbents is given in the table below.

Dates of incumbency	Name	Remarks
1269-1288	Hugo de Dunre	
Installed 1288	Stephen de Montgomeri	
Died 1322	Richard de Dunre	
Not known	Thomas Jynes	
1379-1415	Bartholomew Rous	
1416-1417	John Keole	
1417-1418	John Elye	
1418-?	John Pery	
Late C15 to mid C16	Not known	
Died 1580	Grensill	
1580-1601	Phil Kinwen	
1601-1607	Gabriel Walwin	

1607 - ?	Stephen Boughton	
Died 1659	Mathias Turner	This was at the time of the Commonwealth led by Oliver Cromwell. Parish records were not maintained well.
Died 1692	William Mallowes	
1692-1731	Richard Traherne	Rector of Dyndor with chapel of Rotherwas (Diocesan Institutions, 1923a)
1731-1766	Samuel Bethell	
1766-1800	Francis Brickenden	
1800-1801	Joseph Symonds	
1801-1855	Charles John Bird	Rector of Mordiford and Dyndor (Diocesan Institutions, 1923b)
1855-1897	Rowland Muckleston	Rector of Dyndor only; a different incumbent for Mordiford (Diocesan Institutions, 1923c)
1897-1904	E.C. Phythian-Adams	
1904-1914	Arthur Sumner Walpole	
1914-1927	D'Arcy S. Morton	
1927-1932	Christopher Price	
1932-1942	D. Richard Evans	
1942-1948	Frank N.G. Horth	
1948-1955	John Dent	One Rector for Dinedor and Holme Lacy parishes
1955-1962	Edwin Dunnicliffe	
1962-1966	H.C. Eves	
1966-1973	William Richards	In 1973 the parish of Dyndor became one of six rural parishes in the new South Wye Team Ministry
1973-1984	John Baulch	
1984-1998	Trevor P. Jones	
1998-2006	Peter G. Haddleton	
2008-2014	John Reese	

The Incumbents of Dyndor.[27]
The table is incomplete, especially for the middle years of the 14th century and for about 150 years in the 15th and 16th centuries.

The earliest Rector on record is Hugo de Dunre who served in that capacity 1269-1274 and 'Stephane de Montegomeri' is cited as 'Rector of Dunre' in 1288.[28] Dinedor appears to consist of a single living, although on his gravestone Mathias Turner (died 1659) is described as 'Vicar of Hom Lacie and Parson of Dineder'. Richard Traherne who was incumbent 1692-1731 is described as Rector of Dyndor with the chapel of Rotherwas.[29] In the first half of the 19th century, the incumbent Revd Charles Bird was listed as Rector of Mordiford and Dinedor[30] but when his successor, the Revd Rowland Muckleston, was appointed in 1855, a separate appointment was made for Mordiford.[31] The succession of Rectors listed for Mordiford in the Diocesan Institutions is not the same as those mentioned as incumbents of Dyndor, so it appears that the institution of Revd Charles Bird as Rector for both parishes was unique to his incumbency. (The two parishes are on opposite banks of the River Wye and so an incumbent could not easily pass from one to the other since no bridge across the Wye in that situation has ever existed. Presumably contact was maintained by the use of a simple ferry.)

Little is known about the incumbents prior to the 19th century apart from a memorial in the bell tower extension of the nave to Revd Francis Brickenden who was Rector for 33 years from to 1766 to 1799, when he died. He was outlived for 24 years by his wife, Anne, who is also commemorated.

Revd Charles Bird (1801-1854) and Revd Rowland Muckleston (1855-1897), with their long incumbencies, dominate the 19th century, and had a profound effect on the life of the village and the church. They are good examples of 19th-century philanthropists who enriched the life of their communities by sharing their worldly wealth.

Revd Charles Bird made several contributions to Dinedor, including a handwritten book of information that he had collected concerning Dinedor and Rotherwas. Unfortunately the original copy is held in the Hereford Record Office and, because of the office moving to a new site in 2015, it has proved impossible in recent months to gain access to it.[32] In the 1830s Revd Charles Bird supervised a school and employed a young woman 'to teach the children on the week days and bring them to church on the Lord's Day'.[33] In the vestry is a wooden plaque stating the bequest of £200 by Revd Bird which was invested in 3% consols (a security not limited by a final date), the interest from which was to be used to support the school. Twenty-nine children are recorded as attending for two three-hour sessions, i.e. 9am-12noon, 2-5pm, Monday to Saturday. The success of this venture is seen in the fact that in 1838, out of a population of 301, 169 could read and 90 write and that in the 1840s a school building was constructed. Revd Charles Bird was also a major source of two charitable donations, detailed on a board on the right-hand side of the west wall of the chancel. The first of these was a bakehouse dole of 30 loaves of bread to be given to the poor of the parish on the feasts of the Purification of the Virgin (2nd February) and of the apostle Thomas (21st December) each year. The second donation was of 10 shillings to be given each year on Good Friday to 'poor housekeepers of Dyndor not being in the parish book'.

Revd Rowland Muckleston had been Vice-Provost of Worcester College Oxford University and a notable linguist before becoming Rector of Dinedor.[34] His father was a clergyman who, at the time of Rowland's birth, lived in Lichfield and had several rich livings as well as owning land, so Rowland was already well-off but he seems to have accumulated a considerable fortune of his own, leaving £68,435 at his death, worth c.£6.2 million in 2014.[35] Much of his wealth was used, both during his life and in his will, for a variety of charitable causes. He left his servants the equivalent of £50,000 each and a bequests equivalent to £275,000 to the RSPCA to be used to stop the practice of vivisection. A brass plaque in the south of the chancel of the church records other legacies he made: £1,000 for the village school and to help the poor and needy, and the investment of £10,000 to assist the poorer clergy in the archdeaconry. This investment evolved into the Muckleston Trust which still makes gifts of money to clergy in the area who are in need of financial support. It was during the Rectorship of Revd Muckleston that the church was restored,

Revd Christopher Price,
Rector of Dinedor 1927-32

the Rectory built and the school enlarged (1896). As mentioned above, his grave is near the church porch.

Dinedor had its own Rector until 1948 when Revd John Dent became Rector. From then until 1973, the Rector also had responsibility for Holme Lacy.[36] In 1973 Dinedor became one of several rural parishes which were joined with the parishes of St Martin's and St Francis in urban south Hereford to form the South Wye Team Ministry. From this time there was no Rector for Dinedor apart from the Team Rector, but one member of the clergy team assumed responsibility for conducting most of the services at the church.

Those responsible, and others who helped regularly, are as follows:

Revd Richard Green 1984-88
Revd Rob North 1986-92
Revd Eileen Lloyd 1994-95
Revd Marcia Frampton 1995- 2001
Revd Mark Johnson 2001-09
Revd Iori Price 2008-10
Revd Phil Brown 2009-present
Revd Paul Gill 2011-13
Revd Peter Houghton 2013 - present

The church as a community in recent years

Although in common parlance 'church' denotes the building, theologically the church is the community of worshippers of Jesus Christ. This is understood universally, extending through time and across continents, but also is important in describing a group in a specific locality for a particular time period. Any historical consideration of a church must therefore include its life and activity as a community, regardless of whether that takes place in a consecrated building. An interesting illustration of this from comparatively recent times (2001) is the fact that services continued in the living room of churchwarden Jennifer Smith when the path to the church building was closed because of Foot and Mouth Disease regulations.[37]

Nowadays, the regular services of Holy Communion (held currently twice a month) usually attract a congregation of about ten. From 1995 to 2005 a monthly Family Service was held but this ceased when numbers of children attending dropped. However, special occasions such as Harvest and Christmas services attract many more people. The annual Harvest Festival service sees the church decorated with fruit, vegetables and home-made produce such as jams and chutneys, which are sold off afterwards by auction to raise funds for the church and for charities. A meal together in the village hall is also served and provides a good focus for the village community. Occasional coffee mornings are held to raise funds for the church.

Other community activities in the past have included carol singing around the village, a Christmas entertainment in the village hall and 'safari lunches' where people would process from one house to another, enjoying a different course at each.[38]

Occasionally the church building has been used for special events. On the weekend of 9th and 10th June 1990 a craft exhibition was held demonstrating a variety of skills including lace-making, flower-arranging, embroidery, cross-stitch, crochet and painting. Myrtle Middleton played an important part in organising this and the exhibition attracted the interest of the local press with an article in the *Hereford Times* of 7th June 1990. Photographs are kept in an album available in the belltower near the font.

In 1998 over the weekend 5th to 7th June there was a 'Victorian' celebration to commemorate the 130th anniversary of the opening of the new church. People dressed up in Victorian costume and afternoon tea typical of the period was served.[39]

A special service was held in the church on 1st January 2000 to mark the beginning of the new millennium.

Another photograph album in the belltower records a Festival of Memories which took place in 2008. The path to the church was lined with old bicycles, farm equipment and even an old lorry! Inside the church there was a miscellany of old jars, kettles, garden and farm tools, kitchenware, cameras, washbasins and other crockery.

Occasionally the church has hosted visiting groups.

From 6th to 20th October 1990 a mission was held throughout the South Wye team area and Dinedor hosted five Franciscan monks who assisted with the mission.[40]

On the windowsill on the south side of the chancel is a wooden fish model (see photograph below) given by the St Martin's 4th Hereford Scout Group who made a pilgrimage to the church in May 1995.

On 11th September in both 2010 and 2011 the church hosted a Camp Service for the Hereford Cathedral School Stuart House year 7.

In common with many other villages, it is a long time since the church was a centre of most activities associated with the village and regular attendance is much lower than

The wooden fish given by the St Martin's 4th Hereford Scout Group
to the church in 1995

it would have been in the halcyon days of the last 30 years of the 19th century, after the new church building was opened. It must be borne in mind, however, that at that time larger family sizes coupled with the large workforce needed for farming made for a bigger population, resulting in higher attendance. The absence of alternative attractions is also relevant, although the general decline in Christian spirituality over the last 100 years should not be played down.

Even today however, active members of the parish church are involved in running and participating in several village activities, so the church still plays a significant role in the life of the village.

7 God's Acre

The information given below is copied from a leaflet distributed in 1910 by Revd J.G. Norman to the parishioners:

> I like that ancient Saxon phrase, which calls
> The burial ground God's Acre! It is just;
> It consecrates each grave within its walls,
> And breathes a benison o'er the sleeping dust.

We are much obliged to the Revd J.G. Norman, who thinks the following epitaphs, dated before the beginning of the Parochial Register on April 12th, 1750, may be of interest to any surviving relatives of the persons interred:-

1. On a slab against the North wall of the Tower: 'Mathias Turner, Bachelor of Divinitie, late Vicar of Hom Lacie and Parson of Dinedor, was here interred, Januarie the 13th, 1659.' 'Theodora, the wife of Mathias Turner, was here interred the 15th day of Januarie, 1690.'
2. On the right hand side of the gate, leading from the School and along to the gate leading into the field: 'In memory of Mary, the wife of James Tomkins, who died 15th April, 1735, aged 35.'
3. 'Here lyeth ye body of Elizabeth, ye wife of Thomas Davis, who was buried ye 12th July, 1729.'
4. 'In memory of William Munno, who died August 11th, 1748, aged 72.' 'Also Mary his wife, who died Sept. the 28th, 1744, aged 56.'
5. Next William Munno's headstone an epitaph dated 1720 of which the name of the deceased has mouldered away.
6. A headstone next the gate, leading into the road: 'In memory of the widow [name seems like Vaasher, but almost illegible : probably a foreigner], who departed this life March the 14th, 1721.' On the stone 17 is on one side and 21 on the other. This seems to indicate that the date is 1721.
7. 'In memory of William Ashley, who departed this life December ye 3rd, 1721.'
8. 'In memory of Johny, son of William and Anne Griffith (?), who died ye 20th of May, 1726, aged 3 years.'
9. Against the South wall of the Tower: 'In memory of John Smith, of Much Burch, who died July the 11th, 1733, aged 30.'

10. 'In memory of Ann, the wife of John Preece who died August the 10th, 1717, aged 52.'

11. 'Here lyeth ye Bod   Full Resurrection,
    y of Thomas Lewis Who departed This Life
    In Hopes of a joy   July ye 3, 1707.'

12. A double headstone: 'In memory of John, the son of John Jones, by Mary, his wife, died June 2nd, 1742, aged 11 years.' 'Also Mary their daughter. She died June the 15th, 1742, aged 14 years.' 'Hannah died February the 5th, 1744, aged 6 years.'

At the foot of these lines is another epitaph, extending across the two divisions. It is worded as follows: 'And also Martha, widow of Thomas Baker, of the city of Hereford, who died 5th April, 1833, aged 72 years.'

13. 'In memory of William Davies, who died Sep. 8, 1824, aged 101, also of Mary Davies, his wife, who died Feb. 18, 1835, aged 88.
    Here lies the only comfort of my life,
    The most indulgent husband to his wife,
    The only friend that God did give to me,
    Therefore my loss is great the world may see.'

The above copies have been made as accurately as possible, and the old spelling preserved. But there are other epitaphs, and also verses on the headstones, which have so crumbled away that it is impossible to decipher them. It will be observed that the oldest epitaph discoverable, at present, except those of the Revd Mathias Turner, and his wife, is that of Thomas Lewis, 1707. On further research other interesting epitaphs may be brought to light.

The Revd H.M. Evill will give a Lantern Talk on Church History on Monday, Feb. 21st, at 7, in the Parish Room. I hope earnestly that you will come and hear about your Church and read the leaflet I enclose.

8   Trade and the River Wye at Dinedor

by Heather Hurley

In 1697 Daniel Denell carried out a survey of the weirs, mills, fords and streams of the Rivers Wye and Lugg to ascertain the feasibility of barge trade on the rivers.[1] Describing the conditions downstream from Dinedor he states that: 'the next impediment is a shallow at Hampton bank called Sinkford, this shallow is about 200 yds. in length up and downe the river and in breadth 8 yds. This ford was as we conceive occasioned by the water breaking out of its course there, and overflowing the land and so left ye gravel (that not brought down with ye violence of ye water). In the channel there might easily be a very good passage for vessels of 30 tons and upwards at most times of the year.' Sinkford was on land that now forms part of Sink Green Farm. A short distance away, on the opposite bank of the Wye, was an inn – the Carrots (now Bunch of Carrots) at Hampton Bishop. This was named after a carrot-shaped piece of sandstone seen in the bed of the Wye where the Stank ferry conveyed passengers across the river. A tradition exists that an upturned boat was kept in the orchard and occupied by a tenant who called it Noah's Ark.[2]

Part of the survey carried out in 1697 by Daniel Denell on the navigation of the Rivers Wye and Lugg that relates to the Wye in the vicinity of 'Hampton Bank'

Between 1825 and 1827, the Liverpool & Bristol Company was providing a freight service either by barge, wagon, cart or trolley in the Wye Valley. Timber, planks, poles, bark, boards and trenails were sent to the 'Ship Yard' at Brockweir, Chepstow and Bristol on barges from Mordiford, Sink Green at Dinedor, Hereford, Canon Bridge, Clifford and Moccas together with 'Timber from Hay'. The *Charles*, *Mayflower*, *Eliza*, *John and Mary* and *James* were the barges regularly used by the company for cargoes of timber products.[3]

Dinedor, on the west bank of the Wye, was a parish dominated by the Bodenhams, who resided at Rotherwas in a 'modern and elegant' property with grounds, according to J. Price's *City of Hereford* published in 1796, 'stretching towards the banks of the river, plain and very fertile, crowned towards the south by some gradual ascents, on which are the beautiful woods of Rotherwas: towards the south-west, the view is terminated by the lofty object of Dyndor Camp, from the summit of which are a great variety of prospects of the surrounding country'. Before reaching Rotherwas, the barges passed Dinedor Court with its Boat Meadow and the farm at Sink Green, where sacks of barley, wheat, peas and 'timber from Sink Green' were shipped to Bristol in 1810, a year when coal and lime was delivered on the upstream journey. This trade continued into the 1820s on the *Eliza* captained by William Hoskins, the *Mayflower* and the *John and Mary*, the timber from Sink Green being delivered to Messrs. Watkins in Chepstow.[4]

During the late 18th century Charles Bodenham resided at Rotherwas, which had been rebuilt by his grandfather. Charles, as an appointed proprietor of The Horse Towing Path Company, allowed a section through his land in 1805.[5] Below the house a wharf existed where

A barge passing Rotherwas House

bushels of seeds were unloaded for 'Charles Bodenham Esq.' between 1797 and 1801. Then in 1810 'The Fallage of the greater part of that valuable Coppice called Rotherwas Coppice (Tithe Free), situate in the parish of Dinedor' was auctioned at 'the Hotel' in Hereford, and may have been transported downriver by barge.[6]

Before reaching Hereford the barges passed a wharf at Bullingham where John Knill was shipping sacks of wheat, barley, vetches and ryegrass to Bristol, and Richard Prince was importing coal and lime and exporting '15 Sks of Wheat to Bristol, 14 Sks Barley ditto, 32 Bushel of Oats ditto' in 1810. On the banks of the Wye near the towpath, Joseph Thomas built the *Mary and Elizabeth*, a 46-ton barge, in 1828. A few years later widow Ann Crompton was residing at Bullingham and sold the *William*, a barge of 43 tons, to James Ward of Bishopswood in 1833. For the bargees and hauliers, masters and men there was the Nag's Head kept by Mrs Rosser for drink and shelter.[7]

On the north bank of the Wye opposite Bullingham is Tupsley on the outskirts of Hereford. From the early 1700s the Woodhouse family of merchants had an association

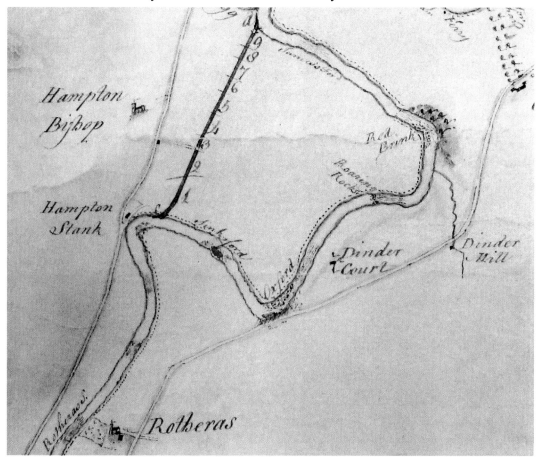

Robert Whitworth's map of 1779 showing the Wye at Dinedor and Rotherwas. Sinkford is shown near the centre of the map. The numbered section was a proposed 'cut' to shorten the route, but it never materialised.

with this area. Barge-loads of coal were discharged at Tupsley between 1797 and 1801, either at the Lower Boat field or at a wharf over the boundary in St Owen's parish.[8] Both river and road travellers in 1802 would have passed 'a public-house, with a sign so singular in its appearance, that it would be difficult to understand how it could be denominated, if an inscription had not been affixed, signifying that this is the real blade bone of a whale'. The inn was named after this curious bone, which may have been brought by 'one of the boatmen, coming upstream with a barge from Chepstow'.[9]

(This chapter is largely extracted from *Herefordshire's River Trade, Craft & Cargo on the Wye & Lugg* by Heather Hurley and published by Logaston Press in 2013)

9   Paintings including Dinedor Hill by George Robert Lewis

George Robert Lewis was born in London on 27 March 1782 and studied under Henry Fuseli in the schools of the Royal Academy. He painted landscapes at the beginning of his career, but became known principally as a portrait painter after 1820.

He exhibited both the paintings shown here and 12 small harvest scenes set in the same locality, at the Society of Painters in Oil and Water Colours in April 1816, announcing them all 'as painted on the spot'. Accompanying each painting were specific titles indicating the viewpoint and giving the time of day that they were painted.

'Harvest Field with Reapers, Haywood, Herefordshire'

'Hereford, Dynedor and the Malvern Hills, from the Haywood Lodge, Harvest Scene, Afternoon'

Lewis, as with many other early 19th-century painters, explored a more naturalistic approach than the previous generation. The apparent truthfulness of their views contributed to the creation of a national identity that was meant to belong to everyone, not just people who owned land. Agriculture had gained in prominence as a result of the Napoleonic Wars when home-based food production had become of national importance, and in these pictures attention is paid to the agricultural work in the scything of the corn, the stacking of the sheaves and the loading of the wagon. These paintings date to the summer of 1815; in 1813 Lewis had toured north Wales with John Linnell, and in 1818 he accompanied Thomas Dibdin on a continental journey. He died in 1871.

10   Rights of Way, Roads and Railways

by Duncan Green

The Wye

Part of our parish boundary is formed by the River Wye, and this would have been one of the earliest 'rights of way'. Various attempts were made to make it navigable, for example by Act of Parliament in 1695 and by the levy of a County Rate, but it has always been problematic due to the large variations in flow. With the advent of the industrial revolution, water transportation became the first choice for heavy loads and various wharves and jetties were constructed on the Wye, including at least one within Dinedor Parish. Large volumes of timber were shipped downstream for shipbuilding, together with cider and agricultural produce, and coal, amongst other items, was brought upstream. For more on the river trade at Dinedor see chapter 8.

Rights of Way

Several of what were once footpaths and tracks have, over time, become our roads as the methods of movement of people and goods have developed and changed. Many more have remained as paths and tracks, since recorded as rights of way, whilst others have fallen into disuse or neglect. Paths that originally existed to enable people to get to and from work, church or school are now mainly used for recreation. Some paths may have started life as 'coffin' routes to the church, by which your bearers on your last journey would have processed on foot to the church.

The National Parks Act of 1948 established a system of Definitive Maps on which were recorded footpaths and bridleways which had a right of way for the public. Under the Act, Dinedor Parish Council was required to submit maps of what it believed to be the rights of way at that time to Herefordshire County Council, who then produced the Definitive Map for the county. It is those footpaths and bridleways, with any subsequent alterations, which are now shown on Ordnance Survey maps.

Not all the rights of way in existence were declared as there were strict guidelines; 'roads', for example, were to be excluded. In addition not all the paths the Parish Council believed to be public found their way onto the Definitive Map. So we are left with anomalies such as paths that terminate on what were deemed 'roads' in 1950 that have since disappeared. These may still be public rights of way, as could other paths which have fallen into disuse or a state of neglect, for 'once a highway always a highway' is a fundamental principle of English law and use of a pathway for many years without restriction (even if without specific permission) is deemed as its dedication by the landowner as a public right. Unless formally closed by legal means (such as through the Magistrates Court) unrecorded public rights of way therefore could well still exist.

Roads

The Public Roads themselves are defined by the 'List of Streets', a statutory document held by the Highway Authority as 'roads maintained at public expense'. Recently this list has been digitised into a map format and is available online.

There are four eras in the development of roads. In prehistoric times the trade in early tools created a network of tracks connecting landmarks, such as hillforts, one to another. (Alfred Watkins, a local man, carried out much research into how landmarks might have been used in the formation of trackways.) Long ridges – which provided for easier passage than following swampy river valleys – played a significant role in the line that such tracks took, as did fords such as those at Hereford and Hoarwithy across the Wye. (The stone bridge at Hereford was built about 1490, replacing a 12th-century timber structure.) With the Romans came engineered roads built primarily for military purposes. These became the basis of our trunk road network, for example the A1 to the north and the A5 London to Holyhead road. In the mediaeval period a growth in trade brought the need for more roads, but the standard of construction was often poor and many were impassable in wet

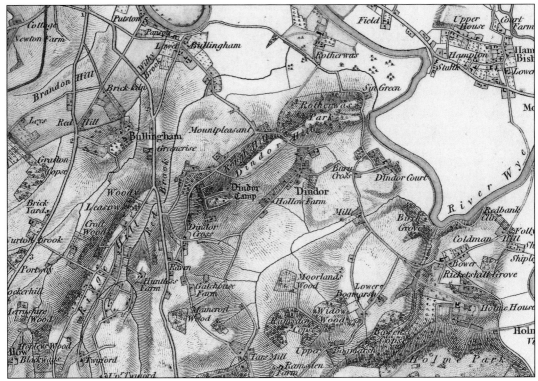

Map of 1831 showing the then road network

weather; many were simply 'made' through continual use. Finally the massive growth in the movement of materials resulting from the industrial revolution coupled with the development of tarmac resulted in more and bigger roads, some of them serving centres on the new canals and railways.

Once a trackway became established its general line would be used over centuries, though its actual course could well vary over time, and this would have been the case in the creation of many of Dinedor's roads. For example, Prospect Lane (or is it Prospect Farm Lane) was an ancient route 'turnpiked' by the Hereford City Turnpike Trust under an Act of Parliament of 1729. Another example is the 'straight mile', but when it was constructed and why is uncertain. It has been reported to have been built by the railways as an accommodation road, but it is not shown on maps drawn when the Hereford to Gloucester railway was built in 1855, nor, surprisingly, is it shown on the plans accompanying the 1863 Act of Parliament authorising the

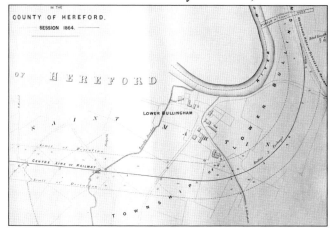

Map of 1864 showing the then proposed 'Hereford curve' for the LNWR, with no indication that the 'straight mile' was then in existence

construction of the 'Hereford curve' for the London and North Western Railway (LNWR). This section remains as the current main line. The straight mile does not appear on maps until the turn of the century and is shown on the 1904 Ordnance Survey map. Very recently a new relief road has been built from the straight mile to the A49, with plans to extend it to the A465. There is also a new cycleway, or Hereford Greenway, which follows the line of the old Hereford to Ross railway.

Dinedor, being so close to Hereford, must have seen the passage of people, goods and much livestock on their way to the city's market. Drovers on their way to London may also have passed through. The main drovers' route from Wales to London was through Erwood, Painscastle, Rhydspence, Hereford and Gloucester, a route which crossed the Wye at Hereford or perhaps Hoarwithy. Dinedor Hill may have been seen as a major landmark to such travellers. Droving peaked around 1830 then declined due to the establishment of the railways.

Under the Highways Act of 1555 (which remained in force for 280 years) each parish was responsible for maintaining its roads. Each parishioner had to provide four days' labour, later increased to six days. Landowners would provide the necessary horses, carts and tools. Nevertheless, by the 17th century the mediaeval roads had generally become mudbaths and travel could be very difficult. With the demand for better roads, and the return of engineering to road-building, money was needed to invest in their construction. This was less of a problem for parishes with only their own local traffic, but how could they finance the through routes? The solution was toll roads, and Dinedor had two!

73

The first English turnpike road was established in 1663 on what is now the A1, created by an Act of Parliament which allowed the collection of tolls. (The word turnpike referred to the early tollgates, which rotated on a spike.) The first Dinedor turnpike road resulted from the Hereford (City) Roads Act passed in 1729 to create a road 'from the said City to Hoar Withy Passage through Holme Lacy being six miles or thereabouts'. A horse ferry existed there. Just a year later, the Hereford City Turnpike Trust for a while became the largest in the country, controlling 118 miles of road.[1]

Because of the problem of pulling heavy wagons over Dinedor Hill to and from Hoarwithy, in 1789 an Act of Parliament was passed to create a new road:

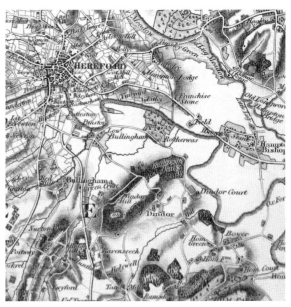

An extract from Henry Price's map of 1817 showing the road across Dinedor Hill now split into Watery Lane and Prospect Lane

> Lower Bullinghope, Rotherwas, Dinedor, Holme Lacey, Ballingham, Little Dewchurch and Hentland which included part of the said Road, now leading from the said City of Hereford through the said Township of Lower Bullinghope over Dinedor-Hill, though the Parish of Dinedor is dangerous and inconvenient to passengers and Carriages on account of the ascent and descent of the said hill, and it would be more commodious and convenient to make a new road through the townships of Lower Bullinghope and Rotherwas, and the parish of Dinedor, to join the present road at or near a place called Bury Cross [now known as Barry Cross].

The old route over Dinedor Hill, clearly once a public right of way as a road, is an example of a road which has fallen out of use and has not made it on to the List of Streets or the Definitive Map.

The remains of the turnpike road over Dinedor Hill with the stone base exposed

Two turnpike routes existed through Dinedor and Lower Bullingham parishes to Barry Cross (then referred to as Bury Cross). One of the cottages at Barry Cross once served as the toll house and a 19th-century milepost still records a distance of 5 miles to Hereford. To the east of the parish, the Even Pitts Ferry was replaced by the Fownhope and Holme Lacy Bridge in 1857.

In the mid 1800s there was major unrest regarding toll roads. In Wales and elsewhere the Rebecca Riots erupted in which men dressed as women attacked the toll gates and toll houses. Partly as a result of the public enquiry that followed, but also because railways were taking the movement of goods and notably livestock off the roads and so reducing the income taken at toll gates making maintaining the roads unviable, by 1865 County Highway Authorities were created and Highway Districts formed to take over the turnpikes. During the 1860s and 1870s Acts of Parliament rescinded the various Turnpike Trusts and the road network became funded through general taxation.

The same period saw the introduction of steam engines on the roads together with traction engines (called locomotives). This resulted in the 1865 Locomotive Act (also known as the Red Flag Act), which provided the right to drive steam engines on the road provided a man with a red flag walked in front. This was the start of the vehicle revolution that continues today. Subsequent Locomotive Acts removed the need for the red flag and increased speed limits, culminating in the Motor Car Act of 1903 which recognised cars as 'Light Locomotives' to provide their right to use the roads.

The 'book of reference' that accompanied the plans for the LNWR's 'Hereford curve' gives the description for the plot of land no.50 on the plans as a turnpike road in the ownership of the Commissioners of the Turnpike Trust.

Railways

December 1853 saw the official opening of the first railways to reach Hereford, from Shrewsbury in the north, and from Newport and Abergavenny in the south. These were quickly followed by the Hereford, Ross and Gloucester railway, a 7 foot 'Broad' gauge which included the 110-yard Dinedor Tunnel. Isambard Kingdom Brunel had originally surveyed the route in the 1830s, but the line was only built by him in the 1850s, construction being held up in January 1853 when the tunnel at Lea was flooded due to heavy rain. Later that year, on 16th April, the *Hereford Times* reported that a workman had received fatal injuries at the Strangford cutting, and on the 30th July a collapse of earth at Dinedor tunnel killed sub-contractor John Baker. The line was finally opened on 1st June 1855, initially serving a temporary station at Barrs Court. Though an independent railway line, it was worked by the Great Western Railway (GWR) and was soon absorbed into its network. In 1869 the GWR converted the line to standard gauge. This is the railway that would have crossed the bridge at the Dinedor end of the straight mile, near Sink Green Farm, where the abutments still remain but the deck has been removed.[2]

In 1861 Hereford was linked by rail to Malvern and Worcester, and in 1866 the LNWR opened a new loop from Rotherwas Junction to Redhill (now the existing main line). This was necessary to avoid through trains having to reverse at Barrs Court. This is the line that crosses the bridge at the Hereford end of the straight mile.

The nearest station to Dinedor was at Holme Lacy, with connections to London Paddington. Ballingham station was added 1908.

Rotherwas was chosen as an ideal site in the First World War for munitions manufacture partly because of these rail links, and the site soon had its own station and engine shed and a substantial network of sidings. It was re-opened in the 1930s and closed in 1964.

The line from Hereford to Ross was closed on 2 November 1964.

Holme Lacy Station around 1910 (© Derek Foxton Archives)

The Future
Study of maps has shown the existence of very old roads in the parish, but there is a need for further investigation on the ground to see what traces of them remain. For example, physical evidence remains of the turnpike road through Dinedor and the original entrance to Dinedor Camp can still be seen. (A simple excavation on the route of the turnpike has shown the stone road base still exists just 6-8 inches below the surface.)

As mentioned above, the old road across Dinedor Hill no longer survives as either a road or even a footpath. If you have any personal evidence of the use of this or other 'lost ways' please contact the Heritage Group, for perhaps these should be added to the Definitive Map.

11 A hundred years of Dinedor occupations, 1851-1951

compiled by Chris Over

Directories and gazetteers are a mine of information for those seeking details from the past, amongst other things they list commerce and businesses located in a given area. Many have been consulted for entries relating to the parish of Dinedor to provide the names of some of those who lived in Dinedor and the businesses they ran.[1] There may be gaps in the information as not everyone chose to be listed in these publications, whilst even directories can make errors in spelling and information – poor old John Coburne got his name spelt in three different ways! Maybe they eventually got it right for Henry (Upper Raven Farm).

The dates quoted reflect the year in which the details appeared in the various publications.

Farms listed with an * appeared in the Rotherwas Estate sale catalogue in 1912 and presumably were occupied by tenant farmers up until that date.

Watery Lane Farmhouse is not at present in Dinedor but is included because much of the land is in the parish and it was also originally part of the Rotherwas estate.

It is interesting to see that between 1885 and 1895 William Lyddiatt farmed both The Glebe and Dinedor Court, at the same time as a Miss Lyddiatt was the schoolmistress. In 1902, Dinedor Cross and Dinedor Mill were run by the same person. It is also interesting to see just how many of the farms changed tenancy after the sale of the Rotherwas Estate in 1912.

Rotherwas House*	Charles de-la-Barre Bodenham, Esq	1858
	Charles de-la-Barre Bodenham, Esq, J.P., D.L.	1876; 1879
	Mrs Bodenham (widow, lady of the manor)	1885
	Mrs Irene de-la-Barre Bodenham together	
	with Count Louis Lubienski J.P.	1890
	Count Louis Lubienski-Bodenham, D.L., J.P.	1895
	Trustees of the late Count Bodenham-Lubienski	1909; 1912

Farming

Blue Bowl	Jacob Brooks	1902
	William Preece	1929; 1937
	Mrs Cobourne	1942

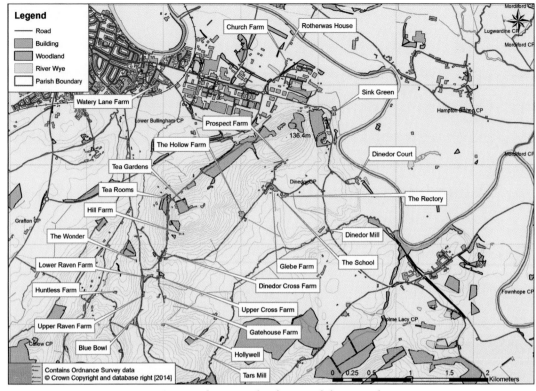

A map showing the farms of the parish

Church Farm, Rotherwas	Dance Bros	1934; 1937
Dinedor Court*	Charles Thomas Bodenham Esq	1851
	Joseph Rawle Paramore	1856; 1858
	Mrs Margaret Edwards	1876
	Felix Ford	1879
	Samuel Bennett	1902; 1909; 1905; 1912
	Roger Mark Williams	1913; 1914
	Langley Shuker	1917
	Joseph Price	1929; 1934; 1937; 1941; 1950
Dinedor Cross Farm*	George Slade	1851; 1856
	William Slade	1858; 1876
	Thomas Froggatt	1885
	William Jones	1890; 1891; 1895; 1900
	John Evans	1905: 1909; 1912
	Thomas John Morris	1913; 1914
	Alfred Nicholls	1917
	Thomas Matthews	1929; 1934; 1937; 1941
	Mrs M. Matthews	1950
Dinedor Cross & Dinedor Mill*	William Jones	1902

Dinedor Court before and after the fire that destroyed many of the old barns in 1972

Dinedor Cross Farm

Dinedor Mill Farm*	George Hiles (miller)	1856; 1858
	William Eaton (miller)	1890
	William Wheatstone (miller)	1876
	Evan Morris	1912
	William Henry Eaton	1913; 1914; 1917
	Thomas Gilbert Eaton	1929
	Miss Elsie Brookes	1934; 1937
	Mr John Thomas	1941; 1950
Gatehouse Farm	William Matty	1876
	James Matty	1890
	John Evans	1913; 1914; 1917
	Alex Evans	1929; 1934
	Alec Ernest Evans	1937; 1941
Glebe Farm	William Lyddiatt	1856; 1858; 1876; 1879; 1902; 1905
	The Misses Sarah & Mary Lyddiatt	1909; 1913; 1914
	Albert Cleland	1929; 1934
	John Cleland	1937; 1941
Glebe Farm & Dinedor Court	William Lyddiatt	1885; 1890; 1891; 1895; 1900
Hill Farm	Richard Stephens	1856; 1858
	Christopher Morris	1876; 1879; 1885; 1890; 1891
The Hollow Farm*	James Jones	1856; 1858
	Charles T. Ockey	1876
	William Jenkins	1879
	Hon. E. Nelson	1890
	Francis Harrison	1891; 1895
	Henry Dan Matthews	1900; 1902; 1905; 1909; 1912; 1913; 1914; 1917; 1929

Gatehouse Farm in September 1973

	Henry John Thomas Matthews	1934; 1937; 1941
	Mr Gilander	1950
Hollywell Farm*	Mr J. Brooks	1912
	Reuben Evans	1937; 1941
Huntless Farm	John Thomas Watkins	1937
Lower Raven Farm*	James Watkins	1876
	Hannah Watkins	1879; 1885
	John Reedy	1890
	Benjamin Morgan	1902
	Messrs Percy & Pryce Jones	1912
	Edward Davies	1913; 1914; 1917
	Arthur Davies	1929; 1934; 1937; 1941
Prospect Farm*	Alfred Oatridge	1876
	John Bridstow	1879; 1885
	John Hart	1890
	Daniel Hart	1891
	Edward Davies	1895; 1900; 1902; 1905; 1909; 1912
	Watts Owen	1913; 1914; 1917
	Mrs Hannah Owen	1929
	Mrs Charlotte Watts-Owen	1934; 1937; 1941; 1950
Raven Farm	George Randal	1851
	Daniel Biggs	1856; 1858
	Benjamin Morgan	1895; 1900; 1905
	A. Davies	1950

Sink Green Farm*	George Langsdon	1851
	(listed as Sin Green)	
	George Meats	1856
	David Yorath	1890; 1891
	John Price	1895; 1900; 1902; 1905; 1909; 1912
	Evan Eustace Jones	1913; 1914; 1917; 1929
	Mrs Evan Jones	1934; 1937
	Mrs Jones & Sons	1941
	Jones Bros	1950
Tars Mill Farm*	William Eaton	1902; 1905
	Henry Eaton	1909
	William Henry Eaton & In Hand	1912
	Jacob Brook(e)s	1913; 1914; 1917; 1929
	Jacob Brookes & Sons	1934
	Godfrey Charles Pritchard	1937
	Alan Greenhowe	1941
	Mr Greenow	1950
Upper Cross Farm	William Edward Morris	1895; 1900; 1902; 1905; 1909; 1912
(no longer a separate farm)	Thomas Price	1914
	Gwylim Owen	1929; 1934; 1937
	John Raymond Pugh	1941; 1950
Upper Gatehouse Farm*	James Mattey	1902
(no longer a separate farm)	H. Tyler & Another	1912
	George Wm. Gregory	1937; 1941
Upper Raven Farm*	Timothy Smith	1851
	John Benbow	1856; 1858
	John Cobourn	1876; 1879
	John Coborn	1885; 1890; 1891
	John Coburne	1895
	Elizabeth Cobourne	1900
	John & Henry Cobourne	1902; 1905
	Henry Cobourne	1909
	J.J. Coburn & Others	1912
	Wm. Edward Morris	1913; 1914; 1917
	Pryce Lewis Morris	1929
	Mrs Mary U. Morris	1934; 1937; 1941
Watery Lane Farm*	William Magness Snr	1876
	James Godsell	1879; 1890; 1891; 1895; 1900;
	(hop and fruit grower)	1902; 1912
	Morgan Watkins	1913; 1917
	Harold P. Goodwin	1937; 1941; 1950
The Wonder*	George Biggs	1890
	Mr George William Gregory	1912
	Mrs Jessie Cobourn (smallholder)	1937

Parish Positions

The Rectory	Revd Charles Philip Tiley (Glebe House)	1856
	Revd W. Bishop M.A.	1851
	Revd Rowland Muckleston M.A.	1858; 1876; 1879; 1885; 1890; 1891; 1895
	Revd Edward Charles Adams M.A.	1900
	Revd Arthur Summer Walpole M.A.	1904; 1909; 1913; 1914
	Revd D'Arcy Strangwayes Morton M.A.	1917
	Revd Christopher Price M.A.	1929
	Revd David Richard Evans M.A.	1934; 1937
Parish Clerk	George Preece	1851; 1856; 1858
	John Gaines	1879; 1885; 1895; 1909; 1913; 1914
Schoolmistresses	Mrs Mary Ann Lyddiatt	1856
	Mrs Mary Ann Smith	1876
	Mrs Alice Magness	1879
	Miss A. Lyddiat	1885 (25)
	Miss Mary Louisa Clarke	1890
	Mrs Anne A. Andrew	1895 (33); 1900 (31); 1902
	Miss Lyddiatt	1929
	Mrs F.E. Bishop	1909 (40); 1913 (36); 1914; 1917

Figures in brackets note average attendance when published.
The years refer to the publication dates of the various directories.

Other Occupations

Note: These people not only lived in Dinedor but carried out their occupations from their homes!

John Gaines	Wheelwright & Blacksmith	1856; 1858
John Gaines	Carpenter & Parish Clerk	1876; 1890; 1902
John Gaines	Wheelwright	1879; 1885; 1891; 1895; 1900; 1937
John Gaines	Wheelwright & Parish Clerk	1905; 1909; 1913; 1917; 1929; 1934
M. Preece	Carpenter	1890
William Wheatston	Miller	1879
William Beavan	Miller (water)	1885
William Eaton	Miller (water)	1891; 1895
Thomas Lewis	Miller (water)	1900; 1905
William Magness	Water Engineer	1891; 1905
William Magness	Whitesmith *(tinsmith)*	1895; 1900; 1905
William Magness	Shoeing Smith	1937
Edwin Wm. Price	Carpenter & Shopkeeper	1890; 1891; 1895
James Mattey	Market Gardener	1895; 1900
Anne Mattey (Mrs)	Market Gardener	1905; 1909; 1913; 1914; 1917
George Jenkins	Market Gardener	1929; 1934; 1937; 1941
Herbert Reynolds	Market Gardener	1929
Mrs Blanche Reynolds	Market Gardener	1934; 1937; 1941
Isles Bros	Butchers	1934

George Nash	Smallholder	1937; 1941
Thomas Moon	Smallholder	1934
William Preece	Smallholder (The Bowl)	1934
William Aspey	Gamekeeper	1851; 1856
William Thomason	Estate Gamekeeper	1890
Thomas Bailey	Cider Retailer	1851
Charles Lawrence	Cooper	1851
John Morgan	Corn Miller	1851
Alfred Outridge	Farmer & Shopkeeper	1851
James Rook	Mason	1851
Samuel Rook	Stone Mason	1856
Samuel Wood	Shoemaker	1851; 1856
Francis Jones	Shoemaker	1856
George Esckley	Haulier	1856; 1858
John Franklin	Nail Maker & Farmer	1891
The Tea Gardens*	William Green	1851; 1856; 1858;
	John Jones	1900
	Francis Harrison	1902
	Frank Harrison	1905; 1909
	Elizabeth Wildman	1912; 1913; 1914; 1917; 1929; 1934
	Jane Holmes	1929
	Leonard Jones	1929
	Louise Holmes	1934; 1937; 1941

(In Kelly's Directory of 1929 three separate tea rooms/gardens are listed)

© Derek Foxton Archives

Population

| 1851 - 250 | 1871 - 283 | 1881 - 263 | 1891 - 270 | 1895 - 270 |
| 1901 - 225 | 1911 - 231 | 1921 - 220 | 1931 - 191 | 1937 - 191 |

12   Dinedor Men in the Great War

by Major David Seeney

BISHOP, Charles William. 14666 Cpl Royal Field Artillery. Born in Shelsey, Worcestershire he was living in Dinedor in 1911. He enlisted at Pembroke and arrived in France 22 July 1915 and served with B Battery, 92nd Brigade. He was killed in action on 21 July 1917 and is buried in Canadian Farm Cemetery, Leper, West Vlaanderen, Belgium. Entitled to the 1914/15 Star, British War and Victory Medals.

BREWER, David. 90383-WR/258552 2nd Cpl Royal Engineers – Waterways and Railways. Born in 1878 in Chorley, Berkshire he married Edith Minnie in 1904. In 1911 he was living at Lanpitts cottage, Dinedor with his wife and son Percy. His trade is given as a platelayer, Great Western Railways. He arrived in France at some date after 1 Jan 1916 and served with a Railway Unit of the Royal Engineers. Entitled to the British War and Victory Medals.

BROOKES, Edgar William. 73098 Sapper Royal Engineers. Born about 1891, son of Jacob and Elizabeth, in 1911 he was living at the Blue Bowl Farm, Dinedor working as a farmworker. He served with No1 Construction Coy Royal Engineers. In 1918 he was living at Tars Farm, Dinedor. No record of overseas service or medals has been found.

COX, John. 2381 Pte Herefordshire Regt. Born about 1874 in Barton St, St Martin's, Hereford. Before 1914 he had served with the Gloucestershire Regt in India, on discharge from which he was employed as a labourer for Mr George Evans, Dinedor. He enlisted soon after the outbreak of the war on 11 September 1914 in the Herefordshire Regt. After serving 182 days he was discharged as medically unfit for war service on 20 January 1915. His next of kin is shown as (Sister) Mrs Rush, Catherine St, Hereford. No overseas service or medals recorded, but he was entitled to the Silver War Badge for discharged servicemen.

DAVIES, Arthur E. 97415 Acting Corporal Machine Gun Corps. Born in 1895 at Blakemere, Herefordshire, son of Edward and Emma Gillah, he later lived at Lower Raven Farm, Dinedor. He served overseas at some date after 1 January 1916, serving with the Machine Gun Command Depot. He was released from military service on 21 January 1919. Entitled to the British War and Victory Medals.

HMS Hecla

DAVIES, Frank Harold. 29655/J68936 RNVR & Royal Navy. Born on 6 February 1899 in Weobley, Herefordshire, son of William and Mary. In 1911 he was living at The Village, Bridge Road, Holme Lacy, Herefordshire. He signed on in the Royal Navy from the RNVR on 27 March 1917 having been a mason's labourer. Served on *HMS Apollo* (Minelayer) and *HMS Hecla*. In 1918 he was living in Dinedor. Entitled to the British War and Victory Medals.

DAVIES, John. Listed on the Dinedor Roll of Honour and the Herefordshire Roll of Honour. Of the many John Davies killed or died in the war, none could be linked with Dinedor.

DAVIES, Harry. 2094/235595 Pte 1/1 Bn Herefordshire Regt. Born in Hereford in 1892 and was living at 20 Holmer Road in 1901. Indentured as an apprentice cooper in 1908. In 1914 he was mobilized with the Herefordshire Regt and is believed to have served in Gallipoli, Palestine and France. He certainly landed at Suvla Bay, Gallipoli on 9 August 1915. During his service he was wounded and gassed, which affected his health and after the war he purchased a cottage and land on Dinedor Hill. Entitled to 1914/15 Star, British War and Victory Medals (see photo).

EVANS, Alex Ernest. G/21708 Pte 1/5 Bn East Kent Regt. Lived at Hollywell, Dinedor. He served in India and was entitled to the British War Medal.

EVANS, Arthur. 3174/233724 1st Gloucestershire Yeomanry and the Corps of Hussars. He lived at Wye Farm, Rotherwas. Served overseas at some date after 1 January 1916. He was released from active service on 2 April 1919. Entitled to the British War and Victory Medals.

EVANS, Reuben Thomas. 1409 Pte Shropshire Yeomanry. Born in Bullingham about 1889, the son of John and Harriette. He farmed at Dinedor Cross and enlisted in the Shropshire Yeomanry Territorial Force on 26 March 1910, attending annual training camps that year and each of the following three. He was called up for war service on 5 September 1914. Released from active service on 8 March 1915 as no longer fit for war service. No record of overseas service or medal entitlement.

GAINES, Joseph Henry. 2364/26949 Pte 2nd Bn Herefordshire Regt and 6 Bn KSLI. He lived at Prospect House, Dinedor. Served in D Company 2nd Bn Herefordshire Regt and overseas service with the 6th KSLI at some date after 1 January 1916. Demobbed on 5 February 1919. Entitled to the British War and Victory Medals.

GAINES, William Ernest. 239164-WR/265116 Sapper Royal Engineers – Waterways & Railways. Enlisted 19 February 1917 and served in France with 262 Railway Company. He was discharged sick and unfit for active service on 26 April 1919 aged 35. Brother of Joseph above. Entitled to the British War and Victory Medals and the Silver War Badge.

HAINES, Henry Roberts. 11704 Pte 5th Bn King's Shropshire Light Infantry. Born in 1885 at Withington, Herefordshire son of Thomas and Mary. In 1914 he resided in Dinedor. Arrived in France on 22 May 1915 and was killed in action in the Battle of Flers-Courcelette, Somme, 17 September 1916 aged 21. He has no known grave and is commemorated on the Thiepval Memorial, Somme. Thomas and Mary Haines were living at the end of the war at Moorfield Cottages, Ocle Pychard. Entitled to the 1914/15 Star, British War Medal and Victory Medals. His parents would have received a bronze memorial plaque with a commemorative scroll and a letter of condolence from Buckingham Palace.

HARRISON, James. 2982 Pte 328 Company - Royal Defence Corps. Home address in 1918 is listed as Rotherwas, Dinedor. He was discharged to the Army Reserve on 4 March 1919. No overseas service or medal entitlement found.

ILES, Charles William. 38845 Pte 1st Bn South Wales Borderers. Born in 1896 at Whittington, Gloucestershire, the son of Charles and Charlotte Sophia. He served overseas at some date after 1 January 1916. In 1918 his address given as Dinedor village. Entitled to the British War and Victory Medals.

JONES, Charles Jones. W/625 Cpl Royal Field Artillery C Battery 122 Brigade (Welsh Artillery – Kitchener's New Army). He arrived in France on 24 December 1915. In 1918 his address is given as Dinedor Cross. Entitled to 1914/15 Star, British War and Victory Medals.

JONES, James. 201227 Pte 1st Brecknockshire Battalion of the South Wales Borderers. He served in East Africa at some date after 1 January 1916. In 1918 his home address was Homend, Dinedor. He was discharged to the Army Reserve on 26 April 1919. Entitled to British War and Victory Medals.

The cap badge of The Herefordshire Regiment in which many of those listed on these pages served

The Memorial Plaque which was given, along with a scroll and a letter from Buckingham Palace, to the next of kin of those serving in the armed forces who died or were killed in the war

The 1914-15 Star (on the left) was issued to all who served in a theatre of war between 5 August 1914 and 31 December 1915 who did not qualify for the 1914 star. Recipients automatically qualified for the British War Medal (centre) which was given to all who served overseas between 1914 and 1920, and the Victory Medal (on the right) which was awarded to all those who served in any theatre of war.

MEREDITH, Charles. Born 1882 in Much Marcle, Herefordshire. In the 1911 census he is listed as a labourer living in Dinedor village with his widowed mother Sarah and brother Joseph, aged 21. He tried to enlist in the armed forces but was rejected as unfit for Overseas Military Service. His address in 1918 is shown still as Dinedor village.

MERTON, Edward S. 43280 Cpl Royal Army Medical Corps. He served as part of the Home Defence with the 2nd Reserve Battalion of the Royal Army Medical Corps. His address in 1918 was given as Dinedor Rectory. Not entitled to any war medals (medals were only awarded for service overseas).

MERTON, Giles. 43278 Pte Royal Army Medical Corps. Served with 17th Field Ambulance. In 1918 he was listed on the Absent Voters list as living in Dinedor. No details of overseas service or medals found. (NB: Edward and Giles's numbers are only two digits apart.)

PERKS, S. A general labourer aged 38 who enlisted under the Lord Derby system (voluntary enlistment pre 1915 before the introduction of conscription in 1916). His home address is given as The Cottage, Dinedor. No military details found, but he is recorded on the Herefordshire Servicemen's Absent Voters list of 1918.

SOUTHALL, Francis Hubert. 2732/235866 1 Bn Herefordshire Regt. Lived at Rotherwas. Arrived in Gallipoli on 1 September 1915 and was taken prisoner of war by the Turks. At the end of the war he was repatriated and discharged from active service on 17 April 1919. Entitled to the 1914/15 Star, British War and Victory Medals.

TAYLOR, John Oswald. 6881 L/Cpl Hertfordshire Regt & 2nd Lt 5th Bn Bedfordshire Regt. Born in 1889, the son of James and Mary Elizabeth Taylor of Rotherwas Park. He arrived in France on 4 February 1917 and was killed in action on 19 April 1917 aged 28. No known grave, but is commemorated on the Arras Memorial. Entitled to the British War Medal and Victory Medals. His next of kin would have received a bronze memorial plaque and commemorative scroll together with a letter from Buckingham Palace. After the war his father was recorded as living in Monmouth.

THOMAS, Stanley. Listed as died on the Herefordshire & Dinedor Rolls of Honour. Of the many men of this name no link could be found with Dinedor.

TYLER, Charles F. Pte 2791 1st Bn Herefordshire Regt, 235885 KSLI, 87913 Royal Defence Corps. Born in Callow in 1887, the son of Edwin and Sarah. In 1911 he was living on Dinedor Hill. He enlisted on 28 October 1914, arrived in France on 6 July 1915, and was discharged with wounds on 16 April 1919 aged 22. Entitled to 1914/15 Star, British War and Defence Medals.

WOOD, William Oliver. Pte 1013/235087 1st Bn Herefordshire Regt. Born in Rhymney in 1894, in 1911 he was living at 5 Springfield Place, Green St, Hereford, working as a coal cutter. In 1914 he was living at Mill Cottage, Dinedor. He landed with the Herefordshire

Regt at Suvla Bay Gallipoli on 9 August 1915, serving with D Company. In the *Hereford Times* of 11 December 1915 he was reported as wounded and a prisoner of war of the Turks, being interned in Kiangi, Turkey. At the end of the war he was repatriated and discharged from active service on 16 April 1919. Entitled to the 1914/15 Star, British War and Victory Medals.

13 Rotherwas Munitions Factory

by Julie Orton-Davies

When the First World War began, Great Britain only had a regular army of 80,000 men and a low arsenal of weapons. In June 1916, to remedy this shortfall, David Lloyd George, who had been Chancellor of the Exchequer, was appointed Minister of Munitions. By April 1916, the Ministry of Munitions had built factories for filling shells in Morecambe, Chillwell (using amatol as the explosive) and Banbury (which used lyddite). A fourth factory was to be built as insurance against loss of production at one of the other factories and to allow for an increase in demand, and as early as January 1916 the *Hereford Times* reported that a munitions factory might be coming to Hereford. Apparently the city council in an attempt to stabilize the level of the local population had already canvassed the Ministry to establish a government controlled factory in the city. Interestingly, Herefordshire was by then the only county not contributing to the munitions industry.

Many of the filling factories were accommodated in existing factory buildings. However, greenfield sites, such as Rotherwas, were also considered and its suitability was based on its level aspect, access to water piped via a 4-inch main from Broomy Hill, gas and electricity for power and lighting, inexhaustible supplies of sand and gravel, together with good transport links in that there was a Great Western Railway (GWR) line which ran from the north-west to the east of the site and a link road that ran through the site. The land was acquired on 15 June 1916, but such was the urgency that the Office of Works had already commenced work on preparing the required 3,000 drawings. The construction contract was awarded to James Mowlem & Co Ltd at £1,200,000 and was signed on 5 July, work having already begun on construction of the rail link by GWR workers. Mr J.F. Milne was employed as the resident architect, and the labour force was drawn from the army itself (around 250 men) together with 500 navvies and 1,500 skilled workers, a category that included architects, draughtsmen, artisans and mechanics.

The Rotherwas site encompassed 545 acres, and was divided into a Northern Section and a Southern Section by the link road, which became known as the Straight Mile, guarded at each end by a gatehouse. The factory supported nine filling factories, seven on the Southern Section which used amatol and two on the Northern Section which used lyddite. It seems that the original plan was to complete the building of one unit on both the Southern and Northern Sections and to begin filling shells. This would allow workers to be trained up

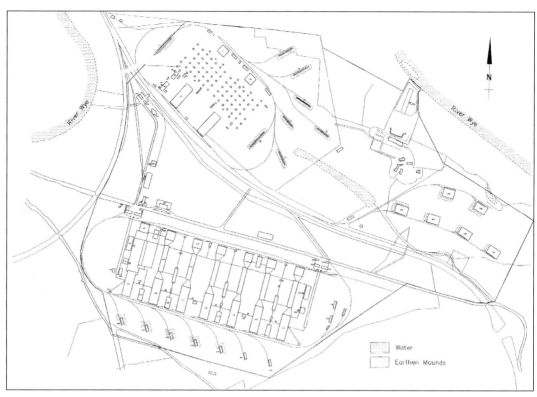

Extract from a map of the site made in 1919 (Courtesy of Herefordshire Lore)

*The construction of the lyddite factory well under way in 1916
— the complex became operational just four months after construction began.*

and enable skilled staff to be transferred to the next units as they came on line. Unit 1 of the lyddite factory filled its first shell on 11 November 1916, exactly two years before the armistice was signed. The first labour return, completed on 20th November 1916, recorded that 142 women and 57 men had been engaged to fill the first shells with lyddite in Unit 1 on the Northern Section. However a redesign of the amatol Southern Section was necessary as a result of a new cold filling process, developed at Woolwich Arsenal. Previously amatol was produced by heating ammonium nitrate (60%) to above the melting temperature of TNT (40%) at which point the two chemicals were mixed. In contrast the new method using 80% ammonium nitrate and 20% TNT, required a milling process, with the advantage of using less TNT whilst producing an explosive with a higher velocity. Unit 1 on the Southern Section was too near completion to be altered and consequently was never included within the cold process programme. However, the building of the remaining six factories (Units 2-7) continued and the large empty building (Unit 1) proved invaluable for accommodating the labourers required to carry out such work. On completion, Units 2-7 were operational as three independent filling factories, each pair supported by an ammonium nitrate store, an ammonium nitrate dryer, a TNT expense store, an incorporation house and pressing/filling facilities. This new method resulted in a delay of nine months, the first shell being produced on the 22 June 1917.

Accommodation, initially for those constructing the factory and then for those working in it, was a problem and in June 1916 the mayor used the *Hereford Times* to announce that there was to be an influx of a large number of workers and that they would need lodgings, urging city residents to offer accommodation.

There is evidence that many of the construction workers came from Ireland and were housed in Unit 1. For example, between July 1916 and the end of 1917, the *Hereford Times* and the *Hereford Journal* contained regular reports of Irishmen being brought before the magistrates court for being drunk and disorderly. This was despite the fact that convictions for drunkenness in Hereford actually dropped during the First World War due to the wartime control of licensing hours which limited opening to between 10.30am and 2.30pm and 6 and 9pm. The nearest hostelry to Rotherwas was the Wye Inn and during the time the factory was being built this establishment was allowed to open for just one hour, at noon each day. Alfred Evans, the son of the then licensee, stated that they had several galvanised baths in the bar which were filled with beer. At 12 noon the navvies came through the door four deep and four abreast, paid their money, picked up earthenware mugs and plunged them into the galvanized baths full of beer. Obviously fighting was an essential, signalled by an empty mug placed upside down as a challenge to any worker. The Wye Inn was also used to supply water in bottles for the workmen who were building the site.

The site was provided with 27 miles of standard gauge railway track, 3 miles of roads, 9 miles of military fencing with 16 sentry posts, 10 miles of footpaths and sentry paths and some 370 buildings, including 3 guard houses manned on a permanent basis. The largest buildings on the site were the nine empty shell stores roughly one acre in size. The design of the empty shell stores and transit sheds on both sections were similar, but many buildings on the Northern side handling lyddite were wooden-framed.

Filling the Shells

Each shell-filling factory comprised an empty shell store and a transit shed for the filled shells, separated by the buildings where the shells were filled. The shells were brought on to the site by GWR rail, entering alongside a platform situated inside the empty shell store, where they were unloaded using an overhead gantry system and positioned in the first one third of the building. The shells were then moved to a central gallery where they were cleaned – rust removed with a wire-brush and any grease washed away. The shells were then painted, with special attention required for the shells to be filled with lyddite (shellac varnish was used as the picric acid would react with the metal to form dangerously unstable picrates). Parts of the bench on which the shells stood during this process would be provided with heating to accelerate drying. Shells then entered a third section awaiting transportation, using the standard gauge railway link, to their designated filling house.

The method for filling shells differed between that used for lyddite and that for amatol. However in both instances the explosives were delivered to the bond stores, positioned some distance away from the production buildings, and then transferred to an expense store prior to delivery to the filling site.

On the Northern Section in the First World War all the buildings were of wooden construction connected by a series of wooden-floored corridors, roofed over and partly walled in. The corridor floors supported a Decauville narrow gauge railway with points and

Workers filling shells in the Northern Section
(Courtesy of Derek Foxton and John Edmonds)

94

turntables. Six bond stores and two expense stores were required to support the two factories on the Northern Section. When required the lyddite/picric acid was removed from the bond store and delivered to the expense store before being processed through a sifting house to remove any lumps. The refined explosive was then loaded into cans and transported to the melting house by way of covered corridors and the internal rail system, where it was placed in an oil tank heated by gas (generated in a gas producing plant situated on the perimeter of the site). The cans were then lidded and delivered to the filling houses, each of which had a lean-to to allow delivery and despatch of shells in the dry. In the centre of the filling houses were a series of melt houses and on the outside were the kit houses holding supplies of beeswax, used to seal the explosive. Each factory supported 22 filling houses and 8 melt houses. Filled and sealed shells were then transported to a transit shed for checking and distribution. Charged shells were sent on to the Pontrilas Ordnance Storage Depot twice daily.

Within the Southern Section the ammonium nitrate stores and TNT bond stores were sited as far as possible from each other, respectively on the southern and northern edges of the site. Before use the ammonium nitrate was brought on site and dried down to a moisture content of 0.4%, placed in round covered tins and taken to the incorporation houses which were set midway between the ammonium nitrate driers and the TNT expense stores. The TNT was delivered by train to the expense store, weighed into 10lb tins

Hand stemming a 9.2 inch shell in Hereford during the First World War. The method was also adopted during the Second World War as it proved to be faster than a mechanical process that was introduced between the wars. There is anecdotal evidence that the Rotherwas process became standard. (Courtesy of Derek Foxton and John Edmonds)

and taken to the incorporation house as required. Incorporation was done using edge runner mills resembling a cider mill but with two rollers: 120lb of ammonium nitrate and 30lb of TNT were placed in the mill, which was then run for 20 minutes. The resulting amatol was then loaded into tins. The filling of the shells was done either manually, known as hand stemming, or mechanically. In the latter method the amatol was taken to a crusher to ensure freedom from lumps, whilst hand stemming required an operative to measure and pour the amatol into an upstanding shell with a funnel, to avoid spillage. Using a stick similar to a broom handle, the explosive was then compacted by hitting the handle with a wooden mallet. Interestingly, hand stemming became the preferred option in both the First and Second World Wars.

The Female Workforce

Recruitment was on a national scale with Labour Exchanges setting up a National Clearing House which matched recruits with factory vacancies throughout the country. Labour Exchanges issued each recruit with a Green Card, which was taken to the designated factory. Hereford received young women from Lancashire, London, Birmingham, south Wales and Ireland as well as all the county's towns.

As early as 1915 the *Hereford Times* was carrying advertisements for women required to work in the munitions industry:

WOMEN OF HEREFORDSHIRE
YOU ARE WANTED NOW
Don't hesitate apply today

The advertisements included contact details for all the towns of the county.

In the following year, 1916, the *Hereford Times* recorded 'ANOTHER URGENT CALL TO WOMEN: The call to women to undertake work on munitions is becoming increasingly urgent ... by March 1917, 80% of all operatives employed must be women ... apply at once to the Employment Exchange nearest to your residence.'

Once the Rotherwas Factory was needing staff, recruitment campaigns took place on Castle Green, whilst 200 Irish girls were personally recruited by a Miss Hogan from Hereford in 1916. They were lodged in Berrington Street and looked after by the Sisters of Charity of St Vincent de Paul until permanent lodgings could be found.

The surge of employment for women principally in munitions factories and on the land during the First World War was to forever change the role of women in society.

Following recruitment the women were trained and after a short probationary period were able to carry out their work well and were mechanically skilled. Their role was to take the place of men and it was a revelation for many that female workers were able to do heavy manual work. Before training the women were paid 15s per week, after training £1 5s, rising to £2 10s with bonuses.

Workers came from all walks of life. Some had not worked before and some could not stand the conditions and left. Requiring a stable workforce, the government therefore introduced The Munitions at Work Act in 1915 which stated that a worker wanting to leave without the consent of the employer was not able to gain employment elsewhere for six weeks. This was enforced by the issuing of a leaving certificate, and applied to both men and women.

A recruitment poster
(Courtesy of Herefordshire Lore)

The Canary Girls

Over the years Herefordshire Lore have recorded the experiences of several factory workers, of whom Annie Slade was one. Annie was born in 1900 and came to Hereford from the Rhondda because she 'wanted to do something for my country.' So she and her friend, Tabitha Rosser, came to work at Rotherwas and lodged with an elderly lady who lived in Whitecross before deciding to move to Ross-on-Wye because they were then nearer home. They travelled from Ross on the WORKGIRL SPECIAL leaving at 6.30am – a special train which travelled from Gloucester six times every day and brought the workers directly into a siding at Rotherwas. The train was full of girls 'singing all the way', according to Annie.

Annie Slade as a young girl (Courtesy of Herefordshire Lore)

On arrival the girls were subjected to a body search:

> We were searched with our own clothes on and then when we went over the other barrier we had to strip off and get searched in our underclothes. Then we had pegs, all with our names, with our clothes hanging on 'em. And our munitions clothes was hung there when we finished. And then we were searched again going out. Yes, for fear we had any powder on us or anything.

Munitions clothes consisted of a suit-like garment with trousers, soft shoes and a hat which had to be tied around the head. (Trousers worn by women were much frowned upon by the general public.)

From her description Annie was working on the Southern Section: 'So when I was in the munitions work I was on the powder.' She described how employees were required to work 12 hour shifts – with two weeks on days followed by two weeks on nights: 'You went backwards and forwards'.

> You had to put TNT and Ammonium Nitrate into the mills and then you had to put on a big board the time you put stuff in and when it had to come out, 'cause if it was over that, it would blow the place to pieces, because the wheels would get too hot.
>
> When we were in the mills, there was a little cart and there was some tins like for you to put all the powder in. Tins would then be taken to the stemming room and let go cold before you could put it in the shells. It could be a couple of days.

Annie explained that when working in the mills it was

> Only us two. Nobody else in there. And we were shut in. It was like secret see and nobody else could go in. And if something went wrong, it was only us two in there. It was very dangerous. But the only thing, with one of us watching the times, the other used to have a five minutes sleep in this cart where the containers was and then we would swap and I'd go and watch the mills and she'd go in.

After two weeks in the mill Annie and Tabitha transferred to the 'stemming room' where the shells were filled. Stemming consisted of compacting the explosive in layers with a broom-like handle which was hammered down with a wooden mallet. Annie owned up to putting notes in the shells for the soldiers before they screwed them down. 'I had a letter back from an Australian fella in the Army.'

When working the mills the girls had to wear face masks. 'There was nothing too hot nor too heavy for us! You had to wear the mask and only show your eyes to see what you were doing. And my hair went all green in the front.'

On nights they would have two breaks in the canteen '... and have a couple of bottles of milk. We had to drink a lot of milk because of the powder. ... and all these Lancashire girls, they'd be step dancing on the tables and we'd be playing the tin plates. They used to wear clogs and change into them when they came into the canteen. I say it was dangerous work but we had fun.'

Annie described the celebrations that broke out on Armistice Day in 1918: 'We were all in lorries in our munitions clothes going around Hereford with the flags.'

Annie returned home immediately after the Armistice and went into service. However, as a result of working at Rotherwas Annie lost all her teeth. 'I had lovely teeth but the powder had gone into my gums.'

Another girl called Jessie Sarah Derry from Ocle Pychard began work at the paint shop in Rotherwas in 1917 and kept a notebook about what she needed to do:

> Enough space should be left between each shell to allow free circulation of air to enable shells to dry quickly. When the shells are dry each one must be painted with two circles, which are known as rings. The upper one must be Green, with a space of 1 inch left from the top of shell. This denotes that the shell contains Exploder - Trotyl. The lower ring is Red and is placed immediately below the green one. Each ring should measure half an inch, so the lower edge of the red ring should be 2 inches from the top of the shell. The red ring denotes that it is loaded and contains lyddite (picric acid). Half inch brushes should be used for 'ringing'.
>
> The next process is stamping the shells. Rubber stamps are used with half inch letters for small shells and three quarter of an inch letters for the large ones. The top stamp is name of shell i.e. 60 P.R (60 pounds) etc.

A studio portrait of Jessie Derry in her munitions clothes. She was awarded the M.B.E. in 1918.
(Courtesy of Herefordshire Lore)

The entry provides evidence of the care and dedication shown by these workers, while the quality and neatness of Jessie's writing offers an insight into the high standard of her education. Her reference to picric acid would suggest that she worked on the Northern Section.

Another source is the diary of Winifred Townsend, who worked at the factory between 1916 and 1918, becoming an 'overlooker' or supervisor for Filling House No. 13 on the Northern Section. There were normally 12 girls in each filling shed and they worked in pairs. Their first task was to fill the shells with boiling picric acid, one filling while the other measured the level with a gauge. As soon as the shell was filled the second pair applied the beeswax from the kit house and inserted the exploder and seal. Winifred records the following in her diary:

Each layer was checked:
Acid half hour checked by Military Examiner
Second fill passed
Third fill passed
Kit passed
TNT exploder bag passed
Complete passed and dispatched

Winifred confirms that she worked 12 hour shifts, two weeks on days and two weeks on nights, being given a compulsory breakfast before starting her shift. Each filling shed completed 300 shells (of various sizes) per shift.

Some of the workers on the lyddite section, including local girl Doris Jones
(Contributed by a family member)

For 17 December 1917 Winifred describes how dangerous the work was: 'I fell with a can of boiling picric acid scolding my eyes, face and both hands. I attended outpatients in Ross-on-Wye for eight weeks, returning to work on the 7th February 1918. I received health benefit of 25 shillings per week.' This compared with her working wage of £2 plus 2s 6d for being an overlooker.

The women came from all over the British Isles and Winifred referred to the Irish girls who worked alongside Londoners. This influx of urban women caused much indignation amongst the local population. The Mayor of Hereford in 1916 declared that 'The City was to be invaded by women, the like of which the City had never seen before.'

The county's middle and upper classes jumped at the opportunity to impose their ideals of morals and living conditions onto the women coming to work at the factory and established the Women Police and Women's Patrol officers 'to save women from their own folly'. Their aim was to rescue fallen women caused by 'high wages and excitement' and they deplored 'the behaviour of some women in the city'.

Some rivalries and tensions arose between the local and the Irish girls as a result of the ongoing troubles in Ireland following the Easter Rising of 1916. While waiting for connections at Barrs Court Station, a local girl was accused of taking an Irish girl's dinner. In retaliation the English girl accused the Irish girl of being a 'Sinn Feiner' and a fight resulted. Later the Irish girls marched through the town carrying banners and shouting 'Ireland forever', as a result of which they were sent home so as to help calm matters locally.

There was also an attempted strike at Rotherwas following the Russian Revolution when Barrs Court Station was picketed by two women. Following an assault upon one of the workers and raising the red flag, Elsie Abel was imprisoned for one month. In her defence it was said that the banner was not red but rather pinkish.

Gabrielle West, who was employed by the factory as a policewoman, wrote the following account of her time:

> May 1917. The amatol section is now working. I never knew such an unruly wild set of hooligans in my life. The new amatol girls are at the bottom of all the trouble. They are recruited in batches of 20-100, some from the Midlands, some from Yorkshire, Ireland, Scotland and Wales. They are brought down here and if accepted are put into very rough hostels and cheap lodgings. Naturally under these circumstances only the roughest of the rough will come, and a good many are girls that have come away from home because they had made things too hot for themselves. Anyhow they are a great trial. They steal like magpies, fight, make up scandalous tales about each other, strike and do their best to paint things red.

Because of her experiences at Hereford, Gabrielle put in for a transfer.

It was a dangerous place to work. Winifred Townsend recalls an explosion in 1917 which killed 43 people.

Two sisters, Ethel and May Phillips, were advised 'to smoke to get rid of the TNT from their lungs'. TNT poisoning, or Toxic Jaundice as it was known to the medical profession, was made a notifiable disease early in 1916. Following this, 430 cases were subsequently notified across all the munitions factories in Britain. At Rotherwas there were 13 cases between 1917 and 1918, including two fatalities: Lily Maud Leaver aged 21 who came from Merthyr Tydfil, and Constance Marion Lotinga aged 20 who came from Hull.

In 1918 the workforce at Rotherwas totalled 5,943, made up of 1,966 men and 3,977 women. After Armistice Day many workers volunteered to leave, glad to go home and resume a domestic life or return to other factory work, 500 returning to the Lancashire cotton mills. Each woman was given two weeks' pay in lieu of notice, a rail pass and a Certificate of Service.

The taking up of occupations by women that had been generally taken by men was only seen by the authorities as a temporary measure, the Dilution Act at the beginning of the war releasing men whose jobs were then assigned to women with the intention that the position would revert to what it had been when the war ended. However, the *Hereford Times* reported some disquiet that women were holding on to jobs much needed by the demobbed soldiers. In their own defence, local girls claimed that they were not robbing any man of work because the jobs did not exist before the war. They stated that they were not all able to take domestic service and the work carried out was not always suitable for the men; 'Girls have to live as well as discharged soldiers.'

The Second World War

At its peak during the First World War the factory employed 6,000 workers. Between the wars the site was used for decommissioning ammunition – all the women had been dismissed leaving 400 men to do the work. In 1932 it was reactivated as a small scale supplementary 'filling factory' to Woolwich, but by January 1937 the decision was made to remove all military explosives from Woolwich Arsenal and transfer all operations to Rotherwas.

In 1938, according to the daughter of a factory worker, 'There was war in the air and the factory was all getting primed ready for it. You could sense it, although dad never told us anything about the factory. You could sense that it was getting primed up.'

Between the wars the filling houses on the Northern Section had been demolished and replaced by 16 large buildings, 8 medium buildings and 1 small building. These replacement filling houses were timber built and protected by rectangular blast walls, each with four entrances. The Northern Section was now primarily used for the needs of the navy to fill torpedoes, mines and depth charges.

Security during both wars was at a premium. Passes had to be produced on entering the site and workers searched before shifts to ensure no metal, jewellery, cigarettes or matches were taken in which might cause an explosion; even chocolate was taken as the sugar could have reacted with the explosive. The First World War's attitude regarding the possession of cigarettes and matches as being 'selfish and unpatriotic behaviour' was reinforced – if caught, instant dismissal was a formality. The First World War had recorded an instance when a women had attacked a factory policeman following a routine search and had been sentenced to one month's hard labour – such was the seriousness of the offence. Workers were also randomly searched before leaving the factory primarily because of petty pilfering. This procedure was not popular with the munition workers as anyone singled out felt they were being victimized.

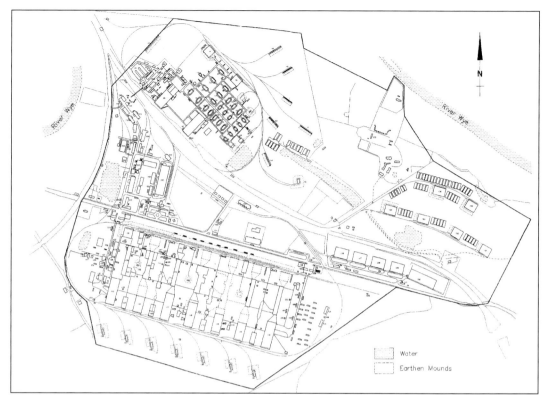

*Plan of the factory in 1942, which can be compared to the aerial reconnaissance
photograph opposite taken by the Luftwaffe in 1940
(Courtesy of Derek Foxton and David Lovelace)*

The wages were still attractive. One worker recalled: 'I was earning 5 shillings a week on the farm and when I went to the munitions factory it was about £3 something. So when I had wages of £3 to £4 I thought I was rich.'

The Southern Section was used for the filling of shells with the Northern Section now used mostly for the needs of the navy. The Northern Section also supported the cordite unit, an area where Nellie Adams earned £1 18 shillings per week weighing and tying cordite. The process was very boring and the substance made the workers very sleepy and so the girls – ten to a table – would sing to keep themselves alert. Nellie also describes how she was forced to take off 13 weeks from her duties because of cordite poisoning, of which the first four weeks were spent in bed. The girls were again working a 12 hour shift: 'If you stopped to think of what you were doing I don't think you could do it. Well you didn't, 'cause we were young.'

Her sister Frances recalls being asked to do an extra shift following the bombing of Coventry in November 1940 because Britain had run out of ammunition with not enough to fire back. Previous to this instance, in the summer of 1940 during the Battle of Britain, Rotherwas was the only factory producing 3.7inch anti-aircraft shells. Truly Britain was living in a very uncertain world and had it not been for the bravery and commitment of national munition workers, the outcome could have been very different.

During the course of the Second World War it was decided to change the shift patterns, and three eight-hour shifts were introduced called Red, White and Blue. This was done to improve efficiency, each worker still having to complete a shift cycle. However, management did now allow women with children to exclude the night shift to help accommodate the needs of family life.

Shells were checked at every stage during the filling process, a task undertaken by the Civil Inspection of Armaments – known as the Top Dogs. Gladys Phillips joined the factory in 1941 and was trained as a CIA examiner, earning £5 per week. She wore a different uniform to the rest of the workforce, consisting of a white overall, beret and red armband with CIA written in white. Gladys travelled by bus to and from the factory and was picked up at the end of her road. She worked in the Northern Section and explained that as an examiner she was in possession of her own personal stamp which she used if the shell was filled correctly. As each examiner had their own stamp, each individual was responsible for ensuring that the shells were safe and fit for purpose, and as mistakes could be traced back to the stamp holder, great care was taken throughout the inspection process.

She worked at the factory for three years before leaving to get married in 1944, and was allowed to leave because she was marrying a farmer and so would be helping on the land.

Not all the women worked on the factory floor. Nora Davies worked in the office for two years as a work taker (checking incentive bonuses from the figures supplied) and was then approached by a newly appointed Entertainments Manager to become a DJ. The broadcasting team chose and played records for the workers during meal breaks. The factory also welcomed visits from various ENSA concert parties and Nora recalls visits by both Anna Neagle and Gracie Fields who came to entertain the workers during their meal break. Nora had to meet the entertainers and introduce them to the workers, and enjoyed her job very much. She did not wear a special uniform but always wore a black beret to protect her hair from the harmful substances during her many visits around the factory.

Similarly the factory employed drivers, and Jeanne Perkins worked for two years delivering consignments of filled shells to Glascoed and Blockley. She had to record her

An aerial photograph of the factory taken on 21 October 1941
(Courtesy of Derek Foxton and David Lovelace)

times of departure and arrival back in Hereford, and very often if it was too late she would stay overnight at the Straight Mile House. This was situated at the Putson end of the Straight Mile near to the railway bridge and appears to have been the home of one of the factory managers. The drivers worked in pairs and were instructed for security reasons to travel without stopping until they reached their destination. Jeanne also went on secret missions to the coast to collect military personnel and escort them to various places. She did not know their identities and if the journey required a stop-over in London she sometimes stayed at the Ritz. There were also less glamorous assignments, such as taking personnel to the railway station including 'a very nice lad called Howlett' who had performed with ENSA. Jeanne earned around £4 per week and left the factory in 1942.

All the factory workers had to be fed and there were four canteens working continuously throughout the 24 hours. On arrival most women went to the canteen before going on shift and Evelyn Davies, the Assistant Manager, was responsible for providing snacks and meals for all four canteens. She remembers a huge kitchen where they cooked the meals, particularly recalling large pans of rice pudding left soaking. Tea and coffee were at a premium, together with casks of beer and cider. All meals had to be paid for and a van would take Evelyn around to each canteen to check the takings and deliver the cash back to a central safe. She also recalled random searches after shifts and described an instance when one of the canteen staff was discovered stealing a packet of butter and was instantly dismissed.

Another worker said that her shifts in the canteen were happy times. She added that one of her jobs was to sell cigarettes to workers after their shift from a kiosk somewhere in the area of the Straight Mile from which she supplied cigarettes through a small hatch, never seeing faces but recognizing purchasers by their voices.

Air Attack

There are two instances of serious enemy air attack. In the First World War Annie Slade describes a Zeppelin incident. During one night the sirens were sounded and the lights went out, as a result of which many workers were injured and some lost fingers. According to Annie when the lights went out the machines should have been stopped at the same time, and workers were supposed to stay where they were. Unfortunately many of the workers ran outside. From this point the story is taken up by Alfred Evans whose family kept the Wye Inn:

> The girls came out of the factory by the hundreds. They were all in their overalls covered with TNT and picric acid, their hair and hands yellow. It was night and they conveniently fainted outside the Wye Inn. I suppose they had run half a mile or three quarters. That was our excitement during the war.

No bombs were dropped, nor is there any official evidence of this event.

The second incident relates to the Second World War. Clohilda Dickinson explained that factory workers in contact with explosives took it in turns to have a bath once a week. The bathrooms were a great distance from the factory proper and the workers were allowed time to have baths during working hours. On the early morning of 27th July 1942, the leading hand

Clohilda Dickinson (Courtesy of Herefordshire Lore)

had said to Clohilda to take the last bath of the shift, and Clohilda had calculated that by the time she had finished her bath her shift would have finished and so she was walking back to clock-off. It was at this moment she heard the sound of an approaching aircraft. Her first thought was that it was a British pilot returning home and then to her horror she recognized the emblem on the plane and realized it was German. The plane swooped down over the units on the Southern Section, the sirens sounded too late, the bombs fell and he was gone. Clohilda recorded that she had never known how many lost their lives on that day. Two 250 kilogram bombs were dropped. The first killed 17 munitions workers who were just finishing their night shift and injured 24 others. The second bomb ricocheted off the sheds and hit Moorlands, the home of the Munitions Police Superintendent Ernest Hursey. It killed him, his wife Vera, his son Ronald who was home on leave from the RAF, and also their eldest son's wife and mother who were staying with them. The sole survivor was their youngest son Ken, who was 16. He told his story to Nicola Goodwin of BBC Hereford & Worcester on the 70th anniversary of the tragedy in 2012:

It just seems in my mind that everything is still there, time hasn't really stopped the picture of the aircraft coming over and dropping its bombs and them bouncing out of the factory area, along the ground and into our house. That will always remain very prominent in my mind. I had a wonderful childhood at Moorlands, we had a lovely garden, nothing could have been better at the time. On the day of the bombing I was living in a back part of the house because we had visitors and the front bedrooms were used for them. About six o'clock in the morning, a lovely, beautiful morning, the sirens went off but nobody really took any notice. A few minutes later I saw a plane come over, it seemed to disappear but then a few minutes later the noise got louder and I saw it coming in over the factory. I looked out of the window and saw the bomb bays open and two bombs drop out. One landed in the middle of the row of sheds and exploded and the other went into the end shed nearest our house, it was probably 200 yards away. It must have bounced on to something and altered its course until it hit the front of the house. I was petrified for a minute but thought, I've got to tell Mum and Dad, so I started to run down the back stairs and then the bomb exploded. I don't know whether I was knocked unconscious or what but everything was so quiet, there was no noise. I couldn't understand what was happening and then eventually I heard somebody running down Watery Lane shouting 'Is anybody about?' and I said 'Yes' and then they said they were going to get some help. They came and gradually dug me out of the debris. Unfortunately my Mum and Dad were killed and so was my brother who has been in the army for 3½ years and had just come back from Gibraltar on his first leave home.

I wasn't injured at all, I can't work it out. I was thrown on my side on the stairs, I couldn't move and I was trapped there with all the debris on top but I just had a couple of scratches. It's phenomenal really when you think about it as the house was completely demolished – I think somebody was watching over me. I can't feel any anger towards the pilot; he was only doing his job. The only bad feeling that I've had is that there was no anti-aircraft guns at the factory; the tower inside the factory was never used. At the time of the bombing the man who had the key was somewhere else and the ammunition was stored elsewhere too. Had they had guns I'm sure they would have been able to shoot the plane down as it was so low that I could almost see the pilot.

I was 16, 17 that November. I went to live with my uncle and aunt and then joined the navy the following March and was stationed in Northern Ireland as an aircraft mechanic, and that's where I met my wife in 1943 and we got married in 1945. I always wanted to come back to Hereford, it was my home. The site of the house is just a builder's yard now and it's a job to visualise after all of these years where my home was and what it looked like but the memories are still there. My Mum and Dad are buried up at Bullinghope; a beautiful spot for them to look out over the countryside.

The pilot dropped his two bombs inside the factory and it was just fate that it bounced across the ground before it exploded. The Germans were only doing their job, the same as my brother who was a fighter pilot in the RAF. I don't bear them any animosity. It's fate. It's just like me being in the back of the house and not in my normal bedroom. I'm not proud to have survived really. I'd much rather not be proud and to have had my Mum, my Dad and my brothers. It's what fate brought me and I just had to do my best to have a good life afterwards. I try to be positive in everything that I do and that's due to my upbringing. We were an army family and we tried to do things properly and make the best of what we had.

The area around Rotherwas is changing greatly with more houses and factory buildings. If they were ever to remember my Mum and Dad with a named street or a plaque I would be very honoured. It would be really nice to have them honoured and I'm sure my parents would have been very pleased.

On the same morning Gladys Phillips was travelling to work for the morning shift, when Morgan's bus was stopped by the police as it approached Belmont. The bus driver was warned by the police to pull into a layby, when they actually saw the German bomber.

A bomb fragment measuring c.6.5 inches long from one of the bombs
(Courtesy Melvyn Holmes)

Gladys said she did not know how many were killed until years later. There was a press embargo and it would appear little information was ever circulated. In both world wars workers had to sign the equivalent of the Official Secrets Act, and it was during the First World War that parliament passed the Defence of the Realm Act [DORA] in an attempt to defend the country from possible internal enemies and spies. In the words of Annie Slade 'things were very secret there', describing her First World War experience, where workers were very isolated within their own environment and knew little about what went on in the rest of the factory.

Accidents

Throughout both wars there were tragedies as a result of the mishandling of explosives. However, on 30th May 1944 there was an explosion that rocked the whole city. The workers had returned from the Whitsun holiday and it was 7pm when a smoking bomb was noticed. It is thought that a bomb had been sealed before it had fully cooled down, which had caused it to overheat. The 'take cover' warning was broadcast and through the bravery of three men, 800 workers were safely removed from the site before the bomb exploded. The area was dampened down and the fire was thankfully confined to the one building, during which time a further 31 2,000lb bombs exploded.

The bravery of the men who fought the fire for four hours and saved hundreds of lives was rewarded with 34 King's Commendation Awards, nine British Empire Medals, five George Medals, an OBE and an MBE. Miraculously there were only two fatalities, but many were injured. It took a whole month to make the site safe but there was no attempt at this stage of the war to rebuild the damaged shed, workers instead being transferred to other munition factories.

Beyond the Second World War

1945 saw the end of the war with flags flying and dancing in the streets. As one Herefordian recounted:

> There was a wonderful spirit during the war helping each other. It's never come back since. Everybody helped one another you know. But after the war finished it all went back to normal. It was wonderful while it lasted. Odd, isn't it? In adversity everybody sticks together. But once it's finished, everybody forgets. I suppose that's human nature.

Since the ending of the Second World War the site has gradually developed into a thriving business park leaving only part of the Northern Section intact. By 1974 the wooden filling houses on this site had been removed leaving only the blast walls and the ancillary buildings, together with the empty shell store (Unit 1). These buildings were also accompanied by three bond stores and one expense store positioned outside the factory boundary. The site has now been awarded Enterprise Zone status and over the coming years will encourage new business into the city with the opportunity of much needed new employment.

It is hoped that the empty shell store and the adjacent blast walls will be developed into a heritage centre to enable future generations to learn about and appreciate the commitment of these brave munition workers both male and female.

14   The Dinedor Secret Army Patrol, 1940-44

by Major David Seeney

The Secret Army of Britain

Following the evacuation from Dunkirk Great Britain was in real danger of invasion and one of the many plans implemented for the country's defence was the formation of a secret army. The intention was to create small units of men who knew the local countryside well, who would literally go underground in specially built hides should German land forces be about to occupy the local area. They would then emerge behind enemy lines with the task of disrupting communications and lines of supply – notably railways, roads and airfields – together with supply dumps, so helping the regular forces in their attempts to push the Germans back. The task of forming this army was given to Colonel (later General) Colin McVean Gubbins. Starting with very little equipment and no trained men, he was obliged to recruit from the civilian population, focusing attention on those who were familiar with the area or had knowledge of explosives. Some of those recruited were miners, farmers, gamekeepers, poachers and postmen. Attention was initially focused on the areas most imminently threatened by invasion, and then on areas that would help protect the industrial heartland around Birmingham.

The recruits were issued with Home Guard uniforms and were grouped into three regions: 101 Battalion for the north and Scotland, 202 Battalion for the centre of Great Britain, and 203 Battalion in the south of England.

These four to six men Auxiliary patrols, as they became known, were the first of the Home Guard units to be issued with the Tommy Gun and often had first call on other equipment. They were also issued with suicide pills, for fear of what might happen to them if captured by the Germans. The men were trained in explosives and weapons, unarmed combat, sniping, navigation, fieldcraft and First Aid, much of the Herefordshire patrols' training taking place at Holmer Grange, the home of Captain Hughie Hall.

As time went on the underground hides were equipped with beds, tables, chairs, lamps and toilets.

In 1944, after the D Day landings and with the threat of invasion over, the patrols were disbanded, some of these highly trained men being snapped up by the Special Air Service, Army Commandos and the Airborne Forces.

Like the Home Guard they would have been entitled to the Defence Medal after three years service.

The Secret Patrols of Herefordshire

Herefordshire had six patrols which were given biblical names. Adam Patrol operated to the west of Hereford, Abednego Patrol in the Leominster area, Jacob Patrol near Bromyard, Mechach Patrol around Ledbury, Caleb Patrol at Dinedor, and Shadrack Patrol around Ross-on-Wye. They all wore Home Guard uniforms with the 202 arm badge, and a Herefordshire Regiment cap badge. For administration they were part of the 3rd Home Guard Battalion of the Herefordshire Regiment.

If the Germans had invaded, the existence of these patrols would have been well known by the time they reached Herefordshire. The life expectancy before being killed or captured would have been 24 hours, but this would have given the patrols at least a chance to blow up the railways and bridges and other targets in their operational area.

Caleb Patrol. From left to right: John Cleland (of Glebe Farm; died 1976). Leslie James Hoddell (of Lyde Court; died 29th October 1953 when living at Wootton Farm, Wellington). Sergeant Angus Wilson (a Hereford seed merchant who lived at 3 Brooklands, Victoria St, Hereford. He had authority to drive a motor vehicle and draw petrol. He died of natural causes in 1944 and a photograph of his face has been glued to a stand-in). Corporal Denis Howard-Smith (of Aldbourne, King's Acre Road, Hereford; he was promoted to sergeant on 23 September 1944 on the death of Sgt Wilson). John French Ryan (born in Monmouth in 1912, he was a veterinary surgeon who qualified at Liverpool University on 12 December 1938. He had authority to drive a motor vehicle and draw petrol. He later became a director of Hereford Racecourse Co Ltd from 1991 to 1994 and died aged 82 in 1994), and Ernest Tisdale (of the Royal George, Widemarsh St, Hereford). Not shown is C.H. Williams of 74 Baysham Street, Hereford. He was a late addition to the patrol, possibly on the death of Sgt Wilson.

The Dinedor (Caleb) Patrol

Caleb Patrol was led by Sgt Angus Wilson and their hide is believed to have been on Dinedor Hill, which had a view of the railways and Rotherwas Ordnance Factory. The hide is believed to have been discovered by an army officer out with his girlfriend, and as a result the officer was soon posted out of the area, but the fate of the girlfriend is not known. Whether a new hide was built or the original hide retained is also not known, and the location of any hide in the Dinedor area is still a mystery!

Dinedor and District Home Guard

The Dinedor and District Home Guard would have been formed shortly after May 1940 following the national call for volunteers, and in due course formed part of the 4th Herefordshire Battalion of the Home Guard. Their initial purpose was to watch out for parachutists and to report their presence to the relevant authorities as speedily as possible, a role that developed (as uniforms and arms were issued) to directly tackling parachutists along with a wider range of duties. The Dinedor unit may well also have had a role in the defence of the Rotherwas Munitions factory. The Caleb Patrol Auxiliary Unit operated

Dinedor and District Home Guard with cups that they perhaps won in a Home Guard shooting competition. Only some members of the platoon have been identified:
Front row: 4th from left, George Patrick; 3rd from right: Jim Davies
Second row: 2nd from left: H.P. Goodwin
Third row: 3rd from left, Ken Nicholls; on the far right: Mr Pugh
Back row: on the far left, Charles Davies

*The men of Dinedor and District Home Guard outside their headquarters,
the Grafton Inn in Hereford, in about 1943.*

under a separate structure and its activities and members should have been a secret from
neighbours and the local Home Guard platoon, but recent research has shown that such
secrecy may have been poorly kept by the burgeoning bureaucracy that grew alongside the
Home Guard.

15 Anti-Aircraft Guns on Dinedor Hill

by Melvyn Holmes and John Davies

A Lewis gun

A Bofors anti-aircraft gun

During the Second World War a platoon from the South Wales Borderers attached to the Royal Artillery set up an anti-aircraft gun emplacement on the southeastern corner of Dinedor Camp. The post consisted of several wooden huts which provided accommodation for around 30 soldiers under the command of a Sergeant Scott, with the gun position surrounded by sandbags. There was another gun located just along the ridge between the northern end of the Camp and the area of woodland. A third emplacement was constructed at the far north end of the ridge overlooking the River Wye and the munitions factory. These were all initially armed with Lewis guns, but after the lone German raider had bombed the factory (see pp.105-108), the Lewis gun at the northern end of the ridge was replaced, for a short time, with a Bofors gun. Melvyn Holmes, who then lived in the Tea Gardens' cottage next to Camp Dairy, later married the daughter of one of the serving soldiers.

Towards the end of the war the huts and gun emplacements were taken down by German prisoners of war. The concrete foundations were broken up and used on various tracks that led down from the hill towards Watery Lane. John Davies, who then lived at Camp Dairy (now Camp Cottage), recalls that he and his older sister Jean used to 'travel from our home in the lorries, sitting in the front between two of the Germans – who apparently used to say to us "My girl, my boy, my girl, my boy". They also

The ship in a bottle made by a German PoW for John Davies

used to make us toys out of old tin cans and bits and pieces. One made me a very good ship in a bottle with my name on the bow of the ship – which I still have.'

16   A Brief History of Dinedor School

compiled by Mike Price

It is reported in *A History of the Royal Society: With Memoirs of the Presidents* by Charles Richard Weld (1848) that one of the Royal Society's early Presidents, Sir John Hoskyns, Bt of Harewood, Herefordshire, who was born in 1733, received his early education from his mother before being sent 'to Dinedor School, and thence to Westminster, where he was a scholar under Dr. Busby from whom 'tis most remarkable he never received a blow'! The history of Dinedor School then goes dark until the 19th century when the first (northern) section of the current building was constructed, probably around 1836.

The 1851 Kelly's Directory for Herefordshire indicates that Dinedor had a Free School supported by the Rector and small fees; its headmistress was Ann Meredith. Dinedor must have been a flourishing settlement at that time because the next record indicates that in 1868 Revd Muckleston restored the church and enlarged the school so as to provide a parish meeting room, presumably by adding the present southern brick section to the building.

Dinedor School group photo with Revd Muckleston, late 19th century

Dinedor School group photo late 19th century

Dinedor School group photo late 19th century

By the early 20th century the outlook was not so good for Dinedor School and Herefordshire County Council's Education Committee's minutes of July 1920 recorded that Dinedor School numbers had decreased. As a result the assistant teacher was replaced

Dinedor School group photo early 20th century

Dinedor School group photo 1913

by a monitor – usually a senior pupil who could be trusted to keep order and help the children with their daily tasks – at a cost of £15 per annum! The slide continued with a further withdrawal of funds in 1921 and eventually, on 30 September 1921, Dinedor School closed.

Closed it remained until the start of the Second World War when pressure from the locals, in particular Mr Matthews of Hollow Farm, who had been among the last pupils at the school in 1921, resulted in its being reopened on 8 January 1940 with Mrs Herbert as head teacher and 33 pupils. The number of pupils remained quite high through the war years (e.g. it is reported that there were 41 registered – though only 12 present – on 27 July 1943, the day Rotherwas Factory was bombed), but its reprieve was to be fairly short-lived. By 1950 there were fewer than 20 pupils and the lack of sanitation in the toilets was an obvious problem, so a group of locals led by Mr Andrew Price of Dinedor Court proposed that the school be closed again and the children bussed to schools in Hereford. Thus, on 25 July 1951, Dinedor School closed for the last time and with the start of the new school year that autumn the children began being bussed to various schools in Hereford. Miss Vaughan wrote in the school log book for 25 July 1951, 'Today we close the school'.

Dinedor School group photo 1946
Seated, left to right: Albert Hall, Richard Townsend, David Price, Mervyn Price,
David Bailey, David Baker
Standing, left to right: Ronnie Birch, Pamela Davies, Miss Vaughan (teacher), Roy Birch,
Sally Rolf, Carol Price, Kitty Bailey (largely obscured by Carol Price), Diane Hall,
Jean Price, Mary Bailey, Margaret Evans, Hazel Lewis, Peter Welch, Margaret Wilcox,
Cynthia Yapp and unknown (cropped)

Above: Dinedor School in 2005.
On the extreme left is the boys' toilet
block; the red brick building in the centre
is the original school and the main
building on the right the 'new' school
built in 1895 under the direction of
Revd Rowland Muckleston M.A.
On the left is the dedication stone
of the 'new' school.

Some memories of children (now senior citizens!) who attended Dinedor School follow:

Jean Snell (née Matthews), The Hollow Farm

On 1 September 1939, at the start of the Second World War, I was a 6-year-old pupil attending Bullingham Convent School together with my eldest sister. When the war started the school was closed and the nuns moved to another convent to make way for British troops. Later when the Americans entered the war, they were stationed there.

I can remember the concern and anxiety of my parents with so many children without a school to go to. My mother said 'we cannot let them run wild and perhaps get into mischief'. My father said with some urgency that we must get Dinedor School reopened, which he did. It all happened quite quickly. I can remember that I quite enjoyed the thought of not having to go to school, but with Dinedor School reopened we were soon back at school.

From our home The Hollow Farm, my sister and I could walk to school if the ground was dry and there was no chance of getting our shoes dirty. We would take the short cut,

119

over the stile next to Mrs Pritchard's cottage onto the Glebe ground, across the corner of the field into the churchyard, out of the churchyard through the main gate, through the kissing gate and what seemed a very long path to the school through a second kissing gate at the bottom. The first thing one saw were the children's outside toilets, the boys on the right and the girls opposite. Continuing on to the end of the main building the school entrance and porch was on the left.

After assembly and having our names called for the register, we all had to assemble in lines in the area facing the Vicarage for physical training. I enjoyed this, but being naturally left-handed and being made to write with my right hand when at Bullingham Convent, I found it very difficult when we were told to turn right or left; this problem has remained with me to this day.

Mrs Herbert was our head teacher. She drove to school with her youngest daughter, Stephanie, in a small car from her home at St Martin's; her eldest daughter, Mary, was at the Girls High School in Hereford. We had student teachers from time to time, for work experience I would imagine.

There was one large school room, light and airy. The children were grouped according to age, the older children on the Vicarage side of the room moving down to the lower age group on the side of the church. There were two large windows on either side of the room, with window sills high enough so that the children could not see out.

The infants were in an area off the main school room. The Revd Evans who lived at the Rectory with his wife and daughter, Christine, took the whole class for religious study once a week.

Children evacuated to stay with families in the Dinedor Cross area also attended our school.

At break time we played in the area facing the church. We all had $1/3$ pint of milk every day which was free. Although a farmer's daughter, I did not drink cold milk at home and did not enjoy it very much.

At the age of 8 I left Dinedor School and attended the Margaret Alan (Red Cap) school in Hereford. With my brother and sister we walked to the bottom of the Wonder Pitch to catch the bus into the city. Two years later my father died and we moved to Pandy near Abergavenny.

Frances Lea (née Hoskins): Prospect House
Dinedor School was opened up soon after the war broke out. That's when my family moved to Prospect House, which was rented from Mr Jenkins. I was 11 years old. Both my parents worked at the Rotherwas Munitions Factory.

The first teacher was Mrs Herbert, the dinner lady was Mrs Clarke from Dinedor Cross, and the school cleaner was Mrs Wilcox. We also had a cookery teacher once a week, Mrs Williams, and she was very good. There were outside toilets, and if you talked in class you stood out in the porch, not so good in the winter. After Mrs Herbert we had a Mrs Cook and later a Miss Vaughan, very Welsh, and a Miss Stephens, in the infants class room.

When I was 14 I left school but I did look after the infants' class for a short while. Revd Evans came and took a religious class once a week.

It was quite a happy school.

Mildred Carter (née Greenow), Tars Mill Farm

My parents Allen and Sarah Anne Greenow moved from Hay-on-Wye to Tars Mill Farm, Dinedor in June 1940. I attended Dinedor School with my older brother Rees and sister Mary from 1940-1945.

Every day we walked over a mile through all weather conditions. I was 9 when I first started at Dinedor School and 14 when I left. My school days were happy ones although they were war years so every day I walked to school carrying my school bag along with my gas mask as we didn't know if or when to expect an attack from overhead bombing. Whenever we heard the air raid siren at school we would run for cover into the safety bunker.

My teachers were Mrs Herbert, Miss Lloyd and Mrs Cooke. The girls had cooking lessons while some of the boys knitted socks on three needles. Two of the boys I remember were Reginald Webb and my brother Rees. They did manage to knit one pair between them but on the quiet they did get a lot of help from some of the girls. Who knows what happened to the pair of socks!

We were told that the girls were going to play hockey so we needed our own hockey stick. I went home and told my dad and he went and looked in Ramsden Wood for a likely piece to make one out of. I was so proud of my dad's achievement and my new hockey stick and enjoyed every minute of using it.

Every Friday I would take money for the teacher to the Rectory, the vicar then being Mr Evans, who was later succeeded by Revd Horth.

Because of the war Rees was allowed to leave school when he was 13 years old to help dad on the farm. His teacher, Mrs Herbert, sent a letter home saying she was sorry to see Rees leaving school because he was such a good influence on the other boys; he still has the letter with him at Tars Mill Farm.

David Price, Dinedor Court

Aged 4 in 1946 I started to walk to Dinedor School with three cousins – Carol, Jean and Mervyn Price. We used to pick up the slops bucket from Dave Brewer, so we could bring back any food waste for his chickens. In the autumn there would be, he would say, 'an apple apiece' for us. That didn't stop the bigger boys pinching some of Mr Cleland's apples as they crossed the field. Miss Vaughan, the head teacher, would walk over Dinedor Hill every day and was always first there. Miss Hobley, later Mrs Lyons, was the other teacher who came by bicycle from Hereford. We used to have to get past Mr Hall's dog on our journey. He bit my brother Mick once I remember.

In the very heavy snow of 1947 Miss Vaughan never missed a day, but there were some days when no pupils managed to get in. School dinners were delivered from Hereford every day and served on special tables that we had to put out. Mrs Cook, from Turnpike Cottage would serve dinner. After dinner Miss Vaughan would read part of a story which all ages enjoyed. She used to spend a lot of time teaching us reading, spelling and times tables. There was a school/Sunday school outing each year to Barry or Porthcawl. Dave Brewer, who had a good voice, used to come and sing on our bus. The dentist used to come around and frighten everyone, and occasionally the nits nurse came to inspect hair.

Miss Vaughan used to give everyone a Christmas present, a sixpence or an orange or something. I remember a family that lived rough in the buildings at the Hollow Farm who came to school in the clothes they slept in. Miss Vaughan cut the wellies off one boy that he had worn for months without taking them off! We had nature rambles around the village sometimes.

Some of the pupils I remember were Ivy, Mary, Kitty and David Bailey; Roy, Ronnie, Roger and Raymond Birch; Cynthia, Tracy and Enid Yapp; Joan, Barbara, John and Ann Davies; Tommy and Sylvia Wilcox; David and Philip Baker; Tony Owen; Gavin Smith and Grenville Tomkins.

Some of the children remember taking the 11 plus and some passed, but most probably failed since the school had all ages up to 14 in two classrooms. The school closed in 1951 and we were moved to Hereford on a daily school bus. There was much resentment and some of the children, off the Camp particularly, stayed home in protest. I know that when the school closed the majority of the children who went to Hunderton, within a few years, passed the 11 plus. This makes me think that the grounding that we had in the 3 Rs was very good, though maybe not enough to pass exams without the topping up that we had at Hunderton.

John Davies, Camp Dairy

The school buildings were more or less as they were before the recent modification. They consisted of the brick built main building from which a wooden passage led to the smaller older building. The younger children were taught in the original part and the older ones in the newer part. I think everyone went into the larger building for dinner. There was a cast iron stove at the front of each class for heating, with a flap at the top for loading coke or coal and another at the bottom for removing ashes. The teacher must have come in early to get this up and running by 9am when the pupils arrived. I can't remember whether there was a guard, but like the cane, it was a dangerous piece of equipment. There were two outside toilets – one for girls, the other for boys.

Marbles at school

At certain times of year, everyone played marbles and since there was very little flat surface in the playground, rather than flicking the marbles along the ground in the usual manner, we used to play from a standing position and throw the marbles like you would throw a dart and hope to have a direct hit on your opponent's marble – which was difficult. When the school closed and we went to Hunderton School, the throw was adopted as an alternative method and was known as 'Dinedor Plonks'.

Walking to school

When we were walking to school from the top of the hill we had to go through a field that was ploughed in autumn. This annoyed us because we had to walk over the ridges, so we used to stamp on the ridges as we went to and from school to restore our footpath. If it was wet we used to puddle it into mud in selected areas and used to fantasize a scenario where Reg Jenkins, who used to walk up to Dinedor to see his girlfriend, would get trapped in the mud. As far as I know he was never trapped but I expect he used a few choice expressions if he got his nicely polished brogues muddy.

Another field, the one immediately below our house, often had a Friesian bull which, at the time, was a breed notorious for being aggressive. This particular one was fitted with a metal face mask which restricted his vision, enabling people to walk past in relative safety. However, if he lifted his head to the horizontal, we think he could see enough to spot people invading his territory. If he was in the field, my sisters and I would walk quietly along the side of the field, instead of the footpath which ran diagonally across the field, in the hope that we could get over the hedge if he charged. We often had some scary moments before we finally got over the gate into the other field but it never managed to get close to us.

Playing in the bales at Hollow Farm
Sometimes when walking from school we used to call in at Hollow Farm, which was owned by Mr Gilander who seemed quite happy to have ten or so kids wandering through his yards and barns. One barn was filled with hay bales during the summer and we used somehow to climb up to the top layer and then start tunnelling down into the bales by moving them around and making passages through them about two or three layers down until we had developed a substantial maze which we would all crawl around. This could have been very dangerous if the bales had slipped but we didn't consider this at the time and there was no health and safety or risk assessments then carried out on farms.

School dinners
School dinners were delivered from a canteen in Hereford in a van that was probably very similar to that of Mr Jones the butcher in 'Dad's Army'. When the van stopped where the Village Hall entrance is now, about eight of us would walk down to it and the driver would lift out the aluminium containers and place them on the road. When he had got back into the van, we would all quickly line up at the back and rear side of the van and lift one of the back wheels off the ground. When the driver started off, the back wheel would just spin round and when he realised what was happening, he would give a shout and we would all let go and run. After he drove off we would then pick up the containers – one kid each side – and take them into the school.

Bird murderer
One day about five baby birds which had had their heads cut off were found on the floor of the boys' toilet. In spite of prolonged inquests by the teachers, no one admitted to having done this. At this time most of the kids were used to watching the family pig being slaughtered by having its throat cut and chickens by having their necks pulled or their heads cut off with an axe, but even so a lot of them were very upset by this incident.

Getting water from the well
Water for making drinks and washing up etc. was collected by the older boys from a well up the lane, just inside the field. No-one ever bothered about contamination in those days and I expect there was a good population of e-coli in the water. The general rule was to boil the water before drinking, but we frequently drank water from the wells and springs when we were walking around the area.

123

Going for nature walks
Usually in the spring, the teacher used to take us on a nature walk. We most often went up the lane opposite the church entrance gate, turned left at the top and continued until we arrived at Watery Lane. I think we returned the same way.

Music lessons
Periodically a tall thin 'mad-professor-looking' gentleman used to come to the school to teach us music. I think all ages attended this. We all played various types of percussion instrument – I think mine was a triangle. The only thing I remember of this was that he used to write musical notations on the black board and we all had to shout 'Ta Ta TaTi Ta TaTi TaTi Ta Ta' to represent the note lengths.

Reciting tables and alphabet
Every morning the whole of the infant class used to recite the times tables and the alphabet. 'One two is two, two twos are four, three twos are six' etc. The proper way, none of these fancy modern methods.

Fight with Refugees
After the war, there was a family of refugees from London living in some army huts located in the field just outside the village on the left side of the road leading from the village to Hollow Farm. I'm not sure if there was a reason, but one of these lads and David Bailey (I think, who lived in a bungalow on the left hand side of the road just after the railway bridge at the start of the Straight Mile) decided to have a boxing match. This went on for a number of days after school in the near corner of the field opposite the church entrance. I'm not sure who won but it provided some entertainment for the rest of the children who watched from a safe distance.

The Cane
The cane used on errant children seemed to be a round rod taken from the back of a dining chair and was about half an inch in diameter and two feet long. It was generally administered with some force on the backside of the offending child or the palm of the hand.

Michael (Mick) Price, Dinedor Court
When I started at Dinedor School, probably in the autumn of 1948, there were a few others who started with me: Tony Owen, Philip Baker and Sylvia Wilcox come to mind though there may have been others. We were in Miss Hobley's class along with all the other younger children. The older children were in Miss Vaughan's class and I think in total there were fewer than 20 of us in the whole school. At the end of that school year Miss Hobley got married (becoming Mrs Lyons) and left, so the following year we were all together in the one classroom under Miss Vaughan's tutelage. It was an excellent learning environment for the youngest; probably not so good for the oldest.

We walked the mile or so from Dinedor Court to school and on the way stopped to deliver a can of milk to Mr and Mrs Broughton, who lived at the end of our lane, and to pick up a white enamel two gallon bucket from near the gate in front of Mr Brewer's house

(Lanpitts) a few hundred yards from the school. Some days he would leave apples or plums or something his wife had baked, in the bucket for us. On those days he would wait at the gate for us and announce that there was one (or maybe two) 'apiece'. It was years before I found out what 'apiece' meant. Occasionally we would hitch a ride in the bread van and get out when it stopped on the Rectory pitch to deliver bread there.

The school had two rooms, each with a stove, and in the winter the teacher had to keep it stoked with coal. I remember it being quite cold. Miss Hobley had a high desk at the front and the blackboard had the letters of the alphabet arranged in two rows (A to M and N to Z). I still think of the alphabet as two sets of letters. At midday we all gathered in the larger room and ate a hot meal (dinner and pudding) delivered in a van from Hereford in metal containers. I always enjoyed the food. The leftovers were put into Mr Brewer's white bucket and he fed them to his chickens; a very sensible arrangement.

We had a morning and an afternoon break from lessons when we could go out into the schoolyard to play (we also had play time after dinner). The schoolyard was small and would have been covered in grass if it didn't have 15 to 20 children churning it up several times every day. There were two playgrounds each with a lavatory, the girls' being in one playground and the boys' in the other. There was no running water in the lavatories and the boys' urinal simply consisted of a plastered wall open to the sky with a half-tile drain at the bottom running away through a hole in the wall out into Mr Cleland's field. Not all of the urine ended up in the field however, because boys often felt challenged to try to pee over the wall rather than against it, so I expect there was a fairly luxuriant growth of weeds on the other side of the wall.

Occasionally the whole school would set out for an afternoon nature ramble and we would usually go north from the school along the same public footpath by which Miss Vaughan used to come to school each day, and wander among the fields and woods with her pointing out interesting things. I enjoyed those outings and learned the names of lots of flowers and trees. When we got back on at least one occasion I remember the big boys opening the front of the clock and moving the hands forward so when Miss Vaughan got back with the stragglers she said 'Well, look at the time' and unknowingly sent us all home early.

Sometime in the early 1950s my father decided that Dinedor School should be closed; I don't know why he decided that or who else supported him. I don't even know if he was the 'ring leader' or if there were others. But I know for sure that it was not a popular idea in the village, particularly among those from the top of Dinedor, and at school my brother David and I were the focus for the blame. The village was divided on the wisdom of closing the school and I believe there were a few pretty heated meetings in the school, which in those days doubled as the village hall. But the lack of sanitation in the lavatories was undeniable and ultimately ensured the school's closure at the end of the 1950/51 academic year.

Arrangements were made for all of the older children to go to Scudamore School in Hereford and the younger children to go to a new school, Hunderton County Primary School that was being built in Hereford, along with hundreds more all over Britain, to cope with what would become known as the baby boom. Hunderton School opened on 2 May 1950, and we probably started there in September 1951. My uncle Robert, dad's brother, lived in Hunderton at that time and I can speculate that the idea of the Dinedor children going to Hunderton School could have come from him.

Recent use of the building

After the closure of Dinedor School the building was still used for many village events. The photograph below shows a gathering of the Payne family holding a silver wedding anniversary/housewarming celebration in 1987. The picture gives some indication of the interior of the old classroom. The windows were purposefully built high above the floor level to prevent the children from staring outside during lessons!

17   Dinedor Sports, 1936-2012

by Bryan Edwards

Dinedor Sports began in 1936 and was the brainchild of the then vicar's daughter Christine Evans. One day, over the Rectory garden hedge, Christine was chatting to the neighbouring farmer John Cleland. During the course of their conversation, she suggested that something could be done for the children of the parish – an annual treat of some kind. From this, Christine and John formulated the idea of Dinedor Sports, the aim being to bring together the community and raise money to take the children of the parish to the seaside on a day trip, since in those days many had never even seen the sea!

The Rural Deanery magazine of October 1936 reported:

> THE SPORTS on August 31st were a great success, everything went with a good swing; kindly good humour and keen enjoyment marked the whole proceedings. The judges had no easy task, especially in the Fancy Dress Competition and our kind friends, Mrs Perkins, Miss Perkins, and Miss Workman, who adjudicated in this are most warmly thanked for their services.
>
> The Portrait Gallery puzzled its patrons, whose guesses, complimentary to the subjects, were often very wide of the mark. Clock Golf and Ladder Croquet attracted many; the Refreshment Stall and Ice Cream vendor did a roaring trade, and few were allowed to pass the sheep at the entrance without having a guess as to its weight.
>
> As the chief of the Organising Committee is away from home, the exact amount of the proceeds cannot be given in this issue of the magazine.
>
> The Dance which followed was very well patronised and was one of the most enjoyable of those which have been held during the last five years.

The Early Years, 1945-1976

The Sports initially took place in the Rectory garden orchard then moved on to the Rectory field. Later it moved to its current position in the old school field, known initially as simply the school field, since the school was still in use.

The earliest known committee comprised John Cleland, Andrew Price, Reg Jenkins and Tim Davies. They were helped by Powell Thomas, Joe Meale, Stan Arthur, Charlie Baker, Arthur Isles and Dave Brewer. The ladies who organised the refreshments included Nancy Price, Flo Cleland, Eileen Davies and Lottie Isles.

DINEDOR SPORTS

(NEAR SCHOOL)

Saturday, August 3, 1946

AT 2-30 P.M.

CHILDREN'S EVENTS, 2-40 p.m.

	Event	Prizes	1st	2nd	3rd
1	100 Yds. BOYS, 14 years and under, Handicap		3/-	2/-	1/-
2	100 Yds. GIRLS, 14 " " "		3/-	2/-	1/-
3	100 Yds. BOYS, 10 " " "		3/-	2/-	1/-
4	100 Yds. GIRLS, 10 " " "		3/-	2/-	1/-
5	60 YDS. BOYS AND GIRLS, 7 years and under, Handicap		3/-	2/-	1/-
6	SACK RACE, BOYS AND GIRLS		3/-	2/-	1/-
7	WHEELBARROW RACE BOY AND GIRL		4/-	2/-	
8	THREE-LEGGED RACE, BOY AND GIRL		4/-	2/-	
9	SKIPPING RACE, GIRLS		3/-	2/-	1/-
10	OBSTACLE RACE, BOYS AND GIRLS		3/-	2/-	1/-
11	FANCY DRESS, BOYS AND GIRLS 9 years and under				
12	FANCY DRESS, over 9 years, open				

ADULTS' EVENTS, 4-30 p.m.

	Event	1st	2nd	3rd
1	220 Yds. Handicap, MEN	5/-	3/-	2/-
2	SACK RACE, LADIES	5/-	3/-	2/-
3	SACK RACE, MEN	5/-	3/-	2/-
4	THREE-LEGGED RACE, LADY AND GENT	6/-	4/-	
5	WHEELBARROW RACE, LADY AND GENT	6/-	4/-	
6	THREAD-NEEDLE RACE, LADY AND GENT	5/-	4/-	
7	EGG AND SPOON RACE, LADIES	5/-	3/-	2/-
8	POTATO RACE, MEN	5/-	3/-	2/-
9	100 Yrds. VETERANS' RACE, over 50	5/-	3/-	2/-
10	OBSTACLE RACE, MEN	6/-	4/-	2/-
11	PILLOW FIGHT, MEN	10/-	5/-	
12	MUSICAL CHAIRS, 'CYCLES	5/-	3/-	
13	SLOW CYCLE RACE	5/-	3/-	2/-
14	LONG JUMP, continuous, 3d. per jump	5/-	3/-	2/-

7 p.m. TUG-OF-WAR, Men, Entry Fee 1/- per man   £4   £1

      TUG-OF-WAR, Ladies   "   "   £1   8/-

Refreshments, Amusements, Competitions
including Skittling for £1, Air Rifle, Darts, Quoits,
Stepping, Guessing, Pony Rides, Swing Boats.

DANCING in Schoolroom 9-12 midnight. Admission, 2/-

Admission to Ground, **1/6** ; Children and Forces in uniform, **9d.** Cars, **1/-**

Bus leaves St. Martin's at 2 p.m., via Wye Hotel; also picks up bottom of Ridge Hill, returning at 8 p.m.
The Committee will not be responsible for any loss or accident occurring on the ground in connection with the Sports.

The Second World War was declared on 1st September 1939 meaning that the sports for that year were the last ones held before they resumed in 1945 for what was referred to as The Homecoming.

In the early years Dinedor Sports was a much bigger event than it is currently, with a special bus service laid on by the Midland Red to ferry the public from Hereford to Dinedor and back in the evening. The Sports then comprised races for children and adults along with novelty races such as sack, egg and spoon, obstacle and slow bicycle, rounded off with the men's tug of war and men's pillow fight.

Competitions included ladies' ankle, men's knobbly knees, Dinedor beauty queen, hat dressing, fancy dress and a baby show. There was a fair and sideshows, including skittles, darts, quoits, hoopla, rifle shooting and guessing games. Another feature was the balloon race, with balloons being found more than once in France. Other activities included pony, donkey and tractor and trailer rides for children. The indoor competitions were much more limited and comprised the best pie, tart, cake, bread and flower arrangement.

At this time the bar was run by a local publican, the refreshments were organised by the ladies and the ice cream supplied by Morgan's Ice Cream, an old long since gone Hereford ice cream maker.

The tug of war teams were usually made up of young farmers who would make their way to the beer tent for a well-earned drink after pulling their hearts out. On one occasion, after quenching their thirst some decided to view the cookery entries. Unfortunately hunger overcame some of them and the winning fruit pie entry which had been left on show on the bench vanished! When the proud cook returned to take her winning entry home it was gone. The lady became enraged by her loss and, unable to see the funny side, complained bitterly to the committee secretary who had to placate her by paying ten shillings in compensation.

An early poster recently found in the attic of Dinedor Court gives a flavour of the sports in earlier years (see opposite).

The Later Years, 1977-2012

Families became more mobile with the increased ownership of cars and the annual trip to the seaside ended in the late '60s or early '70s to be replaced with a Christmas Party for the children. This consisted of tea, party games and a visit from Father Christmas who ensured every child had a present to take home. The parties took place in the old school which was used as the Village Hall from the mid '50s when the school closed. The only amenity in the building was electricity and this wasn't installed until the '60s; there was no running water, no kitchen, and no proper toilet arrangements. Heating was by the open fire in the main hall. Water had to be carried from Glebe Farm and was heated in an electric boiler used, before the advent of the washing machine, for domestic laundry washing.

The party was predominately a children and mothers event, the only men present usually being the games MC and of course Father Christmas. On one occasion the chairman of Dinedor Sports – who doubled for Santa – decided to treat the mothers to a winter warmer and made a hot punch, the basis of which he said was cold tea, though it also had more traditional ingredients such as fruit, spices and fruit juices. This hot toddy was well received with mums returning for a top up. During the children's games the volume of laughter increased enormously, and not from the children, the chairman failing

Fancy Dress at Dinedor Sports, early 1950s; note the swingboats in the background. First on the left is Margaret Wilcox, 'Build more Homes', next to her is Ros Davies (Morris), 'Scarecrow'. The two well-dressed ladies on the right are the judges, Mrs Watts-Owen and Mrs Evans (with gloves).

Baby Show at Dinedor Sports, mid 1950s

to admit that there may have been a bottle of brandy added; happy days and no-one was driving home!

Sadly the children's parties came to an end in 1989 due to new regulations which prevented the use of the school as a village hall; although with fewer children in the village a party was no longer a viable option in any case.

Dinedor Sports, which funded the parties, now entered a new era focusing on charity donations and fundraising for the soon to be built new Village Hall. Details of charity donations are published each year, the main beneficiaries being Dinedor Church, Holme Lacy RDA and St Michael's Hospice, with many more donations going to various causes voted for at each AGM.

In the first half of the '90s the Sports fundraising efforts went into raising money for the new Village Hall; indeed for two years its sole objective was to raise funds to that end, not only running the sports during the day but also organising an evening Barbecue and Jazz Band. The Sports continued to help the Hall project, at one stage making an interest-free bridging loan to help the hall committee over a financial void. In the year of the Foot and Mouth tragedy the enforced closure of the Hall brought more financial problems which were to some extent alleviated by an extra donation from the Sports fund. The chairman of the Sports committee also organised members and others into working parties to carry out all the painting and decorating, cleaning and supply of equipment so that the Hall could be opened on time.

The Sports now consist of more competitions, both indoors and out, with the emphasis on winning trophies for the best aggregate performances and entries. The indoor competitions have increased in number, with classes for children and adults ranging from best vegetable animal to best photograph, with a broad range of cookery and flower arranging competitions which are changed each year, the high standard of entries being testimony to the domestic and creative capabilities of the ladies (and gentlemen) of Dinedor.

The outdoor competitions consist of most of the traditional country sports events which are illustrated by the modern day programme (see overleaf).

A feature of the sports over the last 30 years or so has been an interval attraction which takes place between the children's and adults' events. These have included a majorette team, dog demonstrations, gymnastic displays, and on one occasion an equine dance group that soon after won acclaim at Wembley Arena, but nothing creates more enjoyment than the now traditional Wibbly Wobbly Races. Alongside the races and competitions there are the stall attractions which have remained more or less the same over the years, with innovations such as a miniature train, bouncy castle, water-powered rocket and many

Ladies Race at Dinedor Sports, early 1960s

others. Unfortunately a lot of these features have been curtailed by massive increases in insurance liability costs over the last decade.

Throughout the years since 1945 there have been four special occasions celebrated on Sports day. In 1977 the Queen's Silver Jubilee was marked with the presentation of commemorative mugs to all the children of Dinedor. In 1995 the 50th anniversary of Dinedor Sports was celebrated, attended by three members of the original organising group – Mrs Flo Cleland, and Andrew and Nancy Price – along with Christine Evans who, well into her 90s by then, was special guest of the day. In 2002 the children of the parish were given a commemorative coin to mark the Golden Jubilee. The 2012 Diamond Jubilee saw every child at the sports presented with a medal by Rob 'Marathon Man' Powel, a Hereford Olympic Torch bearer, who also gave them the opportunity to hold the coveted torch.

This is a brief history of Dinedor Sports from its inception to current times, and many anecdotes and past memories will have been overlooked with 70 plus Sports days gone by. Suffice to say that without the support of the people and friends of Dinedor who tirelessly work each year to give those who come along an experience which is becoming a rarity in modern times, and help raise money for charities, the Sports would be no more. I have chosen to omit the names of many from the past and those of to-day, since remembering one and forgetting another would be unfortunate.

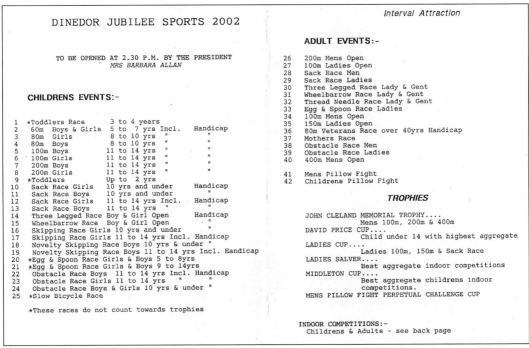

Dinedor Sports programme for 2002

18   Quarries and Stone Buildings

by Paul Thornley

The Herefordshire and Worcestershire Earth Heritage Trust (EHT) is running a three year project (2013-2016) entitled 'A Thousand Years of Building with Stone'. This aims to uncover links between the stone buildings and the quarries where the stone was sourced in a number of locations throughout the two counties. One of these locations is the City of Hereford for some of whose buildings the quarries at Dinedor may well have been a source of stone. This chapter has benefited from research carried out to date on the project, with added input from John Davies (JD) and Tracy Goodwin (TG), in locating disused, overgrown or lost quarries in the area, and identifying buildings in the parish that have been built using local stone.

Before the arrival of the railways, almost all the building stone used in the local area would only have travelled a few miles to be used for the walls and roof tiles of houses, barns and churches. The Old Red Sandstone (ORS) of Herefordshire is very distinctive; an example is the stone remaining in the city walls. Hereford Cathedral was originally built and subsequently repaired from stone brought from the Cathedral Quarry at Caplar and probably also from quarries at Lugwardine and Garnons. Only after the 1850s was stone brought in from Staffordshire, Shropshire and Derbyshire to repair the cathedral.

The fine grained ORS used so effectively in churches at Kilpeck, Peterchurch, Shobdon (the old church) and Leominster was strongly favoured by medieval masons for the rich carvings of doorways, corbels, arches and tympani. The source, or sources, of the stone was undoubtedly local but regrettably now unknown.

Hereford lies by the Wye in a wide river channel containing clay and gravel, so it is to the surrounding terraces and higher ground around that one must look for the quarries. There are two main formations within the Old Red Sandstone in the vicinity of Hereford, produced under different conditions of eroded hills and flowing rivers in a hot dry climate, which resulted in a range of colours, usefulness and abundance. The Raglan Mudstone Formation underlies the central plain of the county; only about 10% of this will produce sandstone in thin bands from which building material can be drawn, the rest being mudstones and siltstones – fossilised soils which form the source of clay used in Herefordshire for bricks, tiles and pipes. Around Hereford, this stone can be seen in the cliffs at Breinton and Holme Lacy and in small quarries at Lugwardine, Hagley, Withington, Lyde and Holmer.

The colour ranges from a dark red-purple colour to brownish-grey and grey-green. The succeeding St Maughan's Formation, which forms the higher ground round Hereford on Dinedor Hill and Ridge Hill in Lower Bullingham, contains a much higher percentage of sandstone and may occur in deeper bands. These bands may also peter out, which can lead to a number of small adjacent quarries. This area is likely to be the source for much of the stone used in Dinedor up to recent times. The stone tends to be pinkish-grey but can be cream-coloured with stripes of purple-red. (The Woolhope Dome to the east of Hereford contains older rocks than the ORS, with large limestone quarries used to source roadstone and some small quarries of older sandstone used for local buildings.)

There are two main sets of public records that provide information about stone quarries and buildings, though they tend to concentrate on historic buildings and existing or recent quarries and give incomplete information on Dinedor parish: Herefordshire Council's Sites and Monuments records (SMR) on the Herefordshire Through Time website[1] and the Strategic Stone Survey sites for Herefordshire (SSSs), undertaken by the EHT for English Heritage and the British Geological Society.[2] The sites identified from these sources were visited, with support from JD, along with those identified from maps and LIDAR. Each entry below starts with its OS grid reference and SMR references are stated for sites where they have been recorded.

Quarries in the Dinedor area

Dinedor Common. Neither quarry listed on either of the above sources.
1. 52082 36560. Steep slope below track, hole, medium-sized quarry (NW facing) partly filled in by village dump, no sign of stone on the surface. Separated by spoil heap (?) from 2.

2. 52080 36591. North of No. 1, lower and a little bigger with less infill, quarry with sandstone exposure (W facing). Hollow was site of JD's uncle's saw bench. Nearby track used for removing wood.

Dinedor Cross. Behind house on SW corner. SMR 40824 and SSSs.
3. 5193 3585. No obvious sign of quarry from side of the road. Possibly filled in at back of the house or overgrown. (Just into Lower Bullingham parish.)

Prospect Lane, near ridge. SMR 40816 and SSSs.
4. 53271 37068. Heading uphill NW along path, sign of excavated slope on RHS of path, and heaps/tumps on LHS of path.

Reservoir overlooking Rotherwas Munitions Factory. SSSs, not on SMR.
5. 53047 37257, top of substantial quarry; 53060 37279, base of quarry. NE, N, NW and W facing. Much evidence of rock from top to base. Fissured, deep bands, clay nodules included. On boundary with Lower Bullingham parish. Area is site of reservoir installed during the Second World War, to fight fires at munitions factory below. Vents, inspection chambers. Spoil-heaps at NW end of area, then levelled area below.

The face of the Reservoir quarry

There is much evidence of earthworks and several small quarries above and below the track to this quarry: at 53142 37265 W facing, 53094 37247 a series of small workings NE facing, 53053 37260 and 52984 37205 a little larger overgrown, NW facing.

Watery Lane, at road track junction. Not on either record.
6. 52925 37234. Small roadside quarry NW facing.

Hollow Farm. SMR 40818 and SSSs.
7. 52920 36650. Faint signs of rough grass on ridge in field.

Blue Bowl, near Hollywell Farm. SMR 40825 and SSSs.
8. 5210 3510. Not seen.

LIDAR mapping of this area was available as part of the Thousand Years of Building with Stone project and gives a very accurate model of the surface with all vegetation removed. It is taken from the air and highlights areas where ground has been disturbed to some depth or excavations have taken place – an indicator of a possible quarry – and can be of great use in heavily wooded areas. This shows clearly the sites of quarries 1, 2, 4 and 5 above.

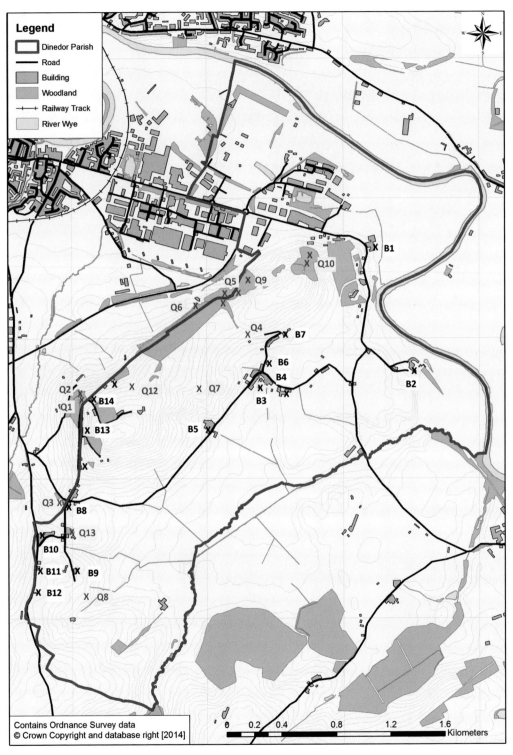

Map showing the quarries (Q) and buildings (B) referred to in the text

In addition it shows large excavations on slopes in woodland on the NE part of Dinedor Hill, sites 9, 10 and 11. None of these are in the two main sources above.

9. 5328 3738. Appears to be larger than the Reservoir Quarry 5. Was this the source of stone for Rotherwas House (though later rebuilt in brick) and Estate?

10. 5375 3756 and 5379 3758, both of them significant size, on the E side of the ridge, one above the other.

11. 5369 3728. SE facing, in the field below the trig point.

TG also identified a stone quarry above Camp Farm, on Watery Lane, Q12, while the site at Upper Cross Farm had a quarry used to provide stone for a barn. This has now been filled in for the new house.

Stone Buildings in the Dinedor area
Buildings mentioned below are those which can be seen to have stone used in their construction when viewed from outside and appear to have been built or restored using local sandstone. Where buildings are rendered, these have not yet been investigated.

From Holme Lacy Road
1. Sink Green Farm at Sink Green, 5417 3763. East side of the farmhouse in stone. West in brick with stone chimneys. Stone boundary walls. (There are also stone garden walls to properties west of the old railway bridge). SMR 47095.

2. Dinedor Court, 5452 3680. Both Court and Dower House are part stone, part brick. SMR 47096.

Dinedor Village
3. Dinedor Church, St Andrews, 5339 3664. West Tower 13th century, stone. The rest completely rebuilt by F.R. Kempson in 1867-8 using coursed sandstone with ashlar dressings outside and ashlar-faced interior.

4. Dinedor Hall, formerly the Rectory, 5357 3660. All in ashlar sandstone, by T. Nicholson 1855. Nearby are the Stables, 5359 3664, now a house.

5. Hollow Farm, 5306 3637. Stone barns and walls. (House rendered). SMR 47097.

On Prospect Lane
6. Bodenham House, 5344 3687, formerly three cottages, the smaller two in rubble sandstone.

7. Prospect Farm, 5352 3702 Two-storey house on slope and single-storey barn attached (now part of the dwelling). All stone.

Dinedor Cross

8. Dinedor Cross Farm, 5199 3586. Stone tower and steps by the side of the road.

9. Upper Gatehouse Farm, 5205 3532. Restored sandstone farmhouse.

10. Lower Raven Farm, 5174 3558. Stone farmhouse restored, stone barns converted to dwellings. SMR 47098.

11. Upper Raven Farm, 5174 3538. Stone barns and outhouses. Farmhouse rendered. SMR 47099.

12. Blue Bowl, 5170 3520. Old stone front to house.

Route to Dinedor Camp/Watery Lane

13. Several newly built or newly restored stone houses, some with old stone walls which appear to be local stone.

14. The Laurels, 52129 36565. Old stone incorporated into house along with several other materials. SMR 48211.

Rotherwas House, SMR 548, 5358 3838. There are records that the house was partially rebuilt in stone in the 16th century. It was then rebuilt in brick, also the remaining buildings and Rotherwas Chapel are in brick.

This chapter is a summary of what is readily obtainable from the records and from observation on the ground, but further research should lead to some additional discoveries regarding lost quarries and their age, and to a more comprehensive account of the stone used in local buildings.

19   History of Sink Green Farm

by Sue Morgan

Sink Green Farm, then occupied by a Mr J. Price and 'another', was purchased by Evan Eustace Jones of Moorhampton Farm, Abbeydore, at the time of the sale of the Rotherwas Estate in 1912. In the sale particulars Sink Green Farm was described as a 'highly fertile & valuable farm', the best on the estate, comprising a stone-built house, farm buildings and rich pasture and arable land extending to over 98 acres with several adjoining pieces of pasture land. The 68 acres of pasture were let at between £192 and £124 per annum. The first bid at the auction was £6,100, and it eventually sold for £7,000.

Evan Jones was a cattle and sheep dealer and he bought the farm to hold stock that he was intending to sell at Hereford Market. The livestock were moved by train from the Brecon and

Aerial view of Sink Green Farm around 1970

139

Sennybridge area to Holme Lacy Station, and then walked to the farm where they were rested before being walked into Hereford. This tradition was carried on by Evan's sons, who often travelled as far as the end of Cornwall to purchase stock.

Evan died in 1935 during the farming depression of the 1930s and his two sons, David Trevor (Trevor) aged 19 and William Stanley (Stan) aged 17, then took over the running of the farm. During the Second World War, Stan, being the youngest, was conscripted into the army, serving in North Africa, the Middle East and Italy, while Trevor ran the farm. The farm was known then as The Green.

Upon leaving school in 1972 Stan's son David worked with both his father and his uncle on the farm, becoming a partner in 1979 just before his uncle Trevor died suddenly, aged only 64. He continued to run the farm alongside his father until Stan passed away in 2009, aged 91. David started doing Bed and Breakfast in 1991, naming the business Sink Green after the original name of the farm. This name probably comes from the fact that the land below the house would have been a flood plain of grass pasture, with very few trees or hedges until the enclosure acts of the 18th and 19th centuries. It was basically a green hollow.

The farm now runs to 170 acres and is bordered by the River Wye, yet is only three miles from the centre of the Hereford.

20   John Gaines (1848-1939)

by Norman J. Owen

John Gaines was born in June 1848 and baptised by the Revd R.H. Dean in St Andrew's Church on 2nd July, when his father entered the family's address as 'the village' and his occupation as wheelwright. In which house John's parents, John and Elizabeth (née Jones), then lived is not known, but it must have been near Prospect Farm, as their entry in the census for 1881 follows that for the farm. John was the eldest child, being followed by Henry, born in 1851, William, who was baptised in October 1852, Elizabeth, who was baptised in December 1854, Susanna Margaret, who was born in approximately 1856 and Sarah, who was baptised in September 1858.

After completing his schooling John became a carpenter and blacksmith, gaining the position of carpenter for the Rotherwas Estate, a post he held for 45 years. During this time he moved into Prospect House, which was an estate cottage that he rented from Mr Charles de la Bodenham and his wife Irene Lubienski Bodenham.

The Banns Register of Pipe and Lyde Church, just north of Hereford, has the following entry for 1872:

> The Banns of Marriage between John Gaines of the Parish of Dinedor, Batchelor and Louisa Ann Burnett of the Parish of Pipe and Lyde, Herefordshire, spinster, were duly published in this Church on three following Sundays viz,
>   The 17th Day of March by Francis T. Havergal
>   The 24th Day of March by T.H. Belcher
>   The 31st Day of March by F.T. Havergal.

The couple were duly married by Revd Francis Havergal on 9th April, John then being 23 years old and Louisa 22, her occupation being given as a domestic servant living at Lyde Vicarage. The pair went on to have seven children, all baptised in Dinedor Church with the exception of John who presumably died at or just after birth: Elizabeth (Lizzie) Mary, baptised in February 1873, John, born in September 1874, Edith Minnie, baptised in May 1877, Joseph Henry, baptised in December 1879, William Ernest, baptised in August 1881, Albert James, baptised in August 1887 and Robert Rowland, baptised in June 1890. Dinedor Church was to play a major role of John Gaines' life, for he filled the role of undertaker, became a bellringer and was also the parish clerk for nearly 67 years. During his period as parish clerk he served under six rectors: R.R. Muckleston, P.C. Adams, A. Walpole, D'Arcy S. Morton, C. Price and D.R. Evans.

When he had become a grandfather and attended church services with his grandchildren, he would dig deep into his pockets and hand out large white peppermints. The children used to go up Dinedor Hill after the service to enjoy tea at the Tea Gardens. He was later quoted as saying, 'In the old days, after the church service, the rector and the farmers who attended would sometimes stand chatting for half an hour. Nowadays it is a question of attending the service and hurrying off home. There is not the happy conversation there once was, and I think all classes have suffered as a consequence.'

John Gaines was noted for his sense of fun. One day, when he was walking to Hereford, he was passed by Revd Muckleston, who was in his pony and trap. The Reverend called to him, 'Gaines, would you like a lift?', to which John replied 'No thank you sir, I'm in a hurry!'

When he was about 60 years old his employment at Rotherwas House must have come to an end but he continued his wheelwright, blacksmithing and carpentry work from his home at Prospect House.

When the Rotherwas Estate was sold by auction at the Green Dragon Hotel in Hereford on 5th September 1912, the estate agents, Edwards, Russell and Baldwin, described Lot 49 (Prospect House) as 'A desirable small holding situated at Dinedor, comprising of cottage with outbuildings, and several pieces of land. Containing in the whole about 2a. 2r. 35p [acres, roods and poles].' The acreage comprised cottage and garden (1.18 acres), pasture (1.084 acres) and another parcel of pasture (0.453 acre), the total coming to almost 2¾ acres. The details also state 'The foregoing is let to Mr John Gaines at a rental of £9.00 per annum'. It is understood that the Bodenham family stated that John Gaines should remain at this property for the rest of his life and, therefore, when the property was sold he should

John Gaines' reredos in Dinedor Church

remain as a sitting tenant. It is believed that John and Louisa used the auction to purchase the smallholding known as Lanpitts for their daughter, Edith Minnie and her husband David Brewer, who were renting it at the time for the sum of £9 12s per annum.

While John was robust and healthy, his wife Louisa did not enjoy good health and had several operations. She was tall and thin and always looked pale and sickly. The villagers

rarely saw her out and about for she spent most of her time around the house. She kept it spotlessly clean, and is remembered for being particularly fussy about the washing up. She was fond of a drink, and when her grandchildren called at the house they would hear the oven door quietly being closed, her brandy or whisky having been hidden away out of sight.

The couple rented an orchard on a slope below the cottage, which had apple, pear, cherry and damson trees. His daughter, Edith, remembers how she used to help gather damsons which were sold to Capel Bevan, a greengrocer in Eign Street, Hereford. In the kitchen-garden John grew raspberries and many vegetables, while redcurrant and blackcurrant bushes grew around the cottage. The couple also kept chickens. When the girls left for their own homes they would always carry home a basket of produce. John and Louisa also 'gave a lot to the church, especially for the Harvest Festival'.

John made his own cider with a cider press that stood by his workshop, using his donkey or a pony to pull the heavy stone crushing wheel. John Gaines also had a trap in which he would often take his family and granddaughter for rides. On one occasion the donkey stopped and refused to go on and despite John's entreaties, he had to succumb to the donkey's wishes and return home.

John Gaines' chair in Dinedor Church

John did a lot of fine carpentry work for the community. He made a reredos for the church which was taken down some years ago and for a long time was left leaning against one of the belfry walls; it is now hanging on the belfry's west wall. He also made a chair for the church which converts into a set of steps from which he could reach the oil lamps. John donated the chair to St Andrew's Church on St Andrew's day in 1901. When John's granddaughter, Edith, married James Frederick Siderfin, John gave them a pair of wooden candlesticks which he had made in his workshop. He also retained his blacksmith's shed next to Prospect House, where his grandchildren loved to watch him work.

In 1667 the only alehouse in Dinedor was suppressed by the Quarter Sessions, and in John's days the Wye Hotel was the nearest inn to Dinedor. For a while it was run by John's brother Henry, and naturally became the local pub. With some of the hotel's customers, John formed a handbell ringing team and at Christmas time they would go around the area playing Christmas carols. John later recalled: 'There were many handbell parties when I was a boy ... and every Christmas, starting on Christmas Eve, we used to make a tour over a wide area. We played at all the big houses – many of them, unfortunately, have since disappeared or are unoccupied, and we were always warmly received.' They would often be invited in for a glass of sherry.

Henry and Myra Gaines, landlords of the Wye Hotel in 1907. Henry was originally a blacksmith and an inventor.

The handbell ringers of the Wye Hotel. Standing from left to right: Henry Gaines, Harold Bull, Mr Preece Sitting: Joe Bundy, John Gaines

Henry's grandson, Alfred Evans, also recalls John performing a Morris Dance at the Wye Hotel with his eldest sons. 'The main bar was cleared of all unnecessary quoits tables etc. so that the dance could be performed. Three spittoons, already brightened with new black lead, were laid equally spaced in a line across the floor. Fresh sawdust was put down and three mops or brooms were supplied. John and his sons danced in hobby horse fashion, weaving in and out of the spittoons, changing direction until the full sequence was completed. The Marquis (a nickname for the local shoe repairer) provided the music on his fiddle to such tunes as "Pop Goes the Weasel".'

In 1932 the *Hereford Times* ran a series entitled 'Old Folk at Home' which featured John and Louisa on Saturday 16th April:

OLD FOLKS at HOME XII -
Dinedor Couple's Diamond Wedding

Up to now, in this series of articles on old folk of Herefordshire, I have confined myself to those who have reached their 90th year, but I do not think it necessary to make an apology for departing from this practice this week to deal with the Diamond Wedding of Mr and Mrs Gaines, of Prospect House, Dinedor, which they celebrated on Saturday. Mr Gaines will be 84 years old in June and Mrs Gaines 83 in November. They were married at Pipe and Lyde Church, and had a family of 5 sons and 2 daughters, 5 of them being still alive. There are 12 grandchildren and 3 great grandchildren.

Mr Gaines, who was house carpenter at Rotherwas House for 45 years, and has since conducted a business as carpenter, wheelwright and blacksmith, has been parish clerk at Dinedor for nearly 67 years, and as long ago as 1921 he was presented with a wallet of notes and an illuminated address in recognition of his services to the church.

The testimonial stated, 'No man has been more closely associated with the joys and sorrows of the people. You have attended nearly every baptism, marriage and funeral, as well as the regular services of the church ... and we make this presentation as a token of our respect and esteem, and trust that your declining days may be full of peace and happiness.'

Louisa and John Gaines

John and Louisa celebrated their diamond wedding at their residence, where there was a large gathering of relatives and friends. Peals were rung on the church bells during the afternoon by sons and a daughter and in the evening there was handbell ringing. Among the messages of congratulations was a telegram from the king and queen, and a letter from Mr J.P.L. Thomas, M.P. in which he hoped 'you have many years of happiness before you'. In fact the couple did not have many years before them, for Louisa died 16 weeks later.

When John was 88 years old he received a presentation. What follows is part of the report from the *Hereford Times* dated 30th June 1936:

For nearly 72 years Mr John Gaines, verger of Dinedor, has rung the bells of his parish church every Sunday to call the people to service from all over the scattered parish. The little parish church was nearly full for the presentation of a photograph, to be hung in the belltower, where he learned his art so many years ago. The rector, the Revd D.R. Evans said John had served his parish church faithfully for nearly 72 years during which time he had only been absent from duty about 12 months all told.

After a long and fruitful life, John died in 1939 at the age of 91. He was buried with his wife in Dinedor Church – the church he loved and served for so many years. The church magazine published the following:

DINEDOR BURIAL

June 17th John Gaines aged 91 years.

It is not given to many to reach the 91st anniversary of their birth. Well very few if any have served as parish clerk and sexton for 74 years. John Gaines lived for 50 years in the house in which he was born on June 10th 1848 and died in the house in which the remaining 41 years were passed. He was a man of many parts, a wheelwright by trade, and a craftsman of considerable skill as is to be seen in the Reredos Screen, the chair in the sanctuary and the clerk's seat in the church. A no mean exponent and performer of the art of handbell ringing. Very ingenious in many ways – he repaired the old clock at Rotherwas Chapel. He was most assiduous and diligent in the discharge of all his duties and all matters connected with the church to which he was most devoted. He remembered the church before the restoration and rebuilding, and it can be truly said he loved it most dearly. Until the last few months he was rarely absent. His was a kindly heart, especially where children were concerned and his memory will be fondly cherished. RIP.

Among the possessions that John left were a horse and dray which he used to transport hay, a horse float which he used for travelling into Hereford for shopping, and a trap which he used on Sundays. His set of handbells hung for several years on the wall at Church House but were eventually sold.

Each of the Gaines family had headstones on their graves at Dinedor but John did not have a headstone put on his wife Louisa's grave. He wanted to wait till after his own death so that the family could include both names. Unfortunately, after his death, his family appear to have squabbled and none of them ever got round to putting a headstone up and the grave of their parents remains unmarked. It seems ironic that a man who did so much for Dinedor lies buried there without a headstone.

The photograph of John Gaines that once hung in the bell tower and now hangs in the vestry

21 The Bishop Family

by Ros Morris

The Bishop family lived at The School House, now known as Brookfield, across the road from the church. Frances Bishop was the schoolmistress at Dinedor School from 1909 to 1921, when she was presented with a silver-plated tea service upon her retirement. She then went on to teach at Bullinghope School. Charles was a gardener for the Lucas-Tooth family at Holme Lacy House. Of their children, Mabel married Jack Price of Green Crize Farm, Lower Bullingham; Gladys married Arthur Davies of Prospect Farm and Lower Raven Farm; Arthur

The Bishop family.
From left to right: Donald, William (Charlie), Mabel, Frances, Gladys, Reginald and Charles

The tea service given to Francis Bishop on her retirement as schoolmistress from Dinedor School

147

was the brother of Bertie Davies who drowned in the Wye while rescuing two other boys. William was a corporal in the Royal Field Artillery who was killed during the First World War (see also page 85). Reginald became an apprentice at RAF Cranwell, where he won many awards for athletics in 1926 before being posted to Egypt. Whilst there he contracted T.B. and was discharged as unfit, only to die from the illness in 1940 aged 32. Apart from the five children shown in the photograph, there was a sixth, Doris, a twin sister of Donald, who died around the age of three.

22   Bodenham House

by Robert Gorman

One hundred years ago the houses at the north end of the village, in the area surrounding the church, could be counted on the fingers of one hand. The main part of the village was based in and around the southern area, Dinedor Hill, almost two miles away.

One of the few houses that existed at the north end of the village was Bodenham House, which dates from the 16th century. In the early to mid-1800s it is believed to have been used as the 'poor house' mentioned on the 'Table of Donations' pictured alongside. This board hung in the school for many years but was moved to the church in 1995 upon the sale of the property. It would have been from Bodenham House that the local poor law commission would also distribute bread to the needy of the village. The interior of the house still contains some wainscotting panelling on the walls, traditionally associated with public buildings of the time.

Bodenham House was originally three separate cottages and gardens (or messuages). At some point the three properties were converted into the substantial house now seen, but clues to its earlier history are still clearly visible.

Bodenham House was part of the Rotherwas Estate and took its name from the Bodenham family who for several hundred years owned Rotherwas, although on some early maps the property is named as Matthews House. The whole estate

Table of Donations due to this Parish. 1820

Nᵒ 1. The Canon Bakehouse Dole consisting of Thirty Loaves of good household Bread; each weighing 1ᵇ 14ᵒᶻ given to the Poor of this Parish, yearly, on or about the Feast of the Purification of the Virgin Mary. Febʸ 2ⁿᵈ

Nᵒ 2. The same Gift repeated on or about the Feast of Sᵗ Thomas the Apostle. Decᵣ 21ᵗ

Nᵒ 3. a Benefaction of Ten Shillings a Year left by the late Mᵣ William Pye of Thruxton. payable on Good Friday, by the Overseer, to the Poor House-keepers of Dynᵉᵈ not being in the Parish Book.

CHARLES JOHN BIRD. A.M. Rectᵣ
ABRAHAM WAINWRIGHT} *Churchwardens.*
WILLIAM PROTHEROE. }

The board in the church listing donations 'due to the Parish' in 1820. The third item refers to a poor house, which is believed to have been the building now called Bodenham House.

Bodenham House in 2014

was put up for auction in 1912; Bodenham House failed to sell and was purchased by private treaty in 1913 by the Misses Sarah Harriett and Mary Jane Lydiatt, spinsters, who at the time resided at Glebe Farm.

23 Cranwell

by Tim Howson

Cranwell was built in 1935 for Albert Cleland of Glebe Farm, a local farmer and land-owner, and grandfather of Dudley Cleland, the current farmer at Glebe. Cranwell was designed by local architects W.W. Robinson & Sons and built in the corner of one of Glebe Farm's fields. Albert's intention was to retire to the new house, but he and his wife Annie never did so.

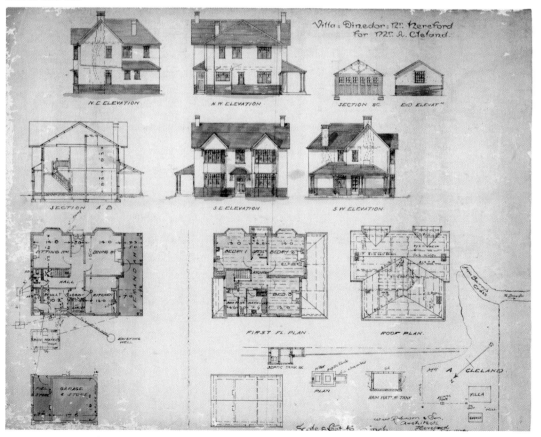

The original architectural plans for Cranwell drawn up in 1935

The house was solidly built of local brick and had many innovative design features not common in 1935. These included a double garage, an underground rainwater collection tank linked to the house, and its own generator.

It was referred to as The Villa on the architects' plans, but was renamed Cranwell as a tribute to two of Albert's sons who had joined the Royal Air Force and learned to fly at the RAF College at Cranwell in Lincolnshire. Albert's youngest son, also called Albert, had been killed in a flying accident, aged 22, in Sudan in December 1932. His eldest son, Ralph, had a distinguished career as a bomber pilot in the Second World War, rising to the rank of Group Captain and being appointed a CBE in 1945. He died as a result of war service in 1948, and is buried in Dinedor churchyard.

The house was rented out until the mid-1950s when it was sold at open auction and bought by John Cleland (brother of Ralph and Albert), also of Glebe Farm. It was rented out again, and one of the longest tenants was the Nash family. They moved out in 1976 and John and his wife Florence (Flo) intended to retire there. However, John's untimely death in 1976 meant that Flo moved in alone in April 1977, living there until her death in 2000. After another period of letting to tenants, the house was sold in 2005 to the current owners Tim and Shelagh Howson, who also, coincidentally, have a background in the Royal Air Force, thus keeping the link with the name chosen by the first owner!

24   The White House

by Ann Morgan (née Phillips) and Frank McGinty

Part One, by Ann Morgan

I moved to Dinedor on 6 November 1959, with my parents and three sisters. I was aged 10; my sisters 8, 3 and 1. My sister Sally and I continued at Hunderton Primary School where we were followed by my younger sisters in due course. Eventually we all passed the 11+ and progressed to the Girls' High School. To get there we caught the school bus with our contemporaries from Dinedor, Rotherwas and Green Crize. I remember the Prices from Dinedor Court, the Prices from Hollow Farm, the Cliftons, Clelands, Hancocks, Walkes, Preeces, Owens, Nicholls, Peytons, Gladwyns, Greenows, and many more all catching the bus to primary and secondary schools.

My father, Harry Phillips, and his friend Alan Peake had bought some land from Andrew Price of Dinedor Court and Albert Hall of The Oaks. They split the piece of land into two and we had the corner plot, amounting to one third of an acre, where my father built a four-bedroomed house. We never decided on a name, and it just became known as the New House or the White House. Alan Peake, with his wife and two daughters, Alison and Katie, built a bungalow called Falconfield on their plot next door. They moved in after us.

I remember on Sundays going to 'help' – we made tea in pint mugs and played as I recall. My dad was a constructional engineer and could do much of the work himself, but also called on the men who worked for him. I don't remember the brickwork being built, but then the bulk of the work was done during the week when we were at school. I do remember the soil being extremely stony, however, for Sally and I were paid 6d a bucket to pick stones out of the soil. This was later doubled to 1 shilling.

I remember Mr Brewer, from Lanpitts, an old cottage on the opposite side of the road, and Mr Roberts who lived at Dinedor Hall (the old Rectory) – Sally and I were often sent to each of them with cakes or pies. I also remember the Nash family who lived at Cranwell. Their children, Penelope, William and Benjamin, went to private schools and were not allowed to use the school bus, but we were all friends nevertheless.

We all went to Dinedor Sports in July. We made gardens on plates, picked bunches of wild flowers and made cakes for the various competitions. Dad guessed the weight of the pig and tried the shooting range. We ran, jumped and hopped through the races and had a great time. Mum even opened the Sports one year!

I remember my days at Dinedor as a time when the whole family were together. Unfortunately, after realising a long-held dream to build his own house, my father died in 1965 at the age of 50. I married and left home in 1968, and Sally left and went to college in 1969. My mother then decided to sell up and move with my other two sisters into town, which she did in 1971. The house was auctioned at the Farmers Club, where it realised £15,100 – a huge amount of money at the time. The new owners, Arnold and Julia Ellis, moved after two or three years, and the house was then bought by the McGinty family, who still live there.

The White House as pictured in the auction particulars in 1971

Part Two, by Frank McGinty

Mr and Mrs Phillips had sold the property to Arnold and Julia Ellis in the early 1970s. Arnie was a businessman and Julia a physiotherapist; they had two daughters and a son. When we bought the White House from them in March 1976, it shared a well with the neighbouring bungalow as there was no mains water. They also both had septic tanks as there were no mains sewers either. The heating, including the central heating, was coal-fired and hard work.

I worked in Hereford as a consultant pathologist until my retirement in 2006, while my wife, Melba, worked as a consultant community paediatrician until her retirement in 2002. Both our fathers helped with the initial work we carried out on the house and garden; indeed, Melba's dad's wall still separates us from the large field behind our home. Later on we had a new garage built, a 'granny flat extension' formed from the previous garage, two new chalets erected and the whole garden revamped. This included landscaping and architectural features such as new gates and pillars and a front wall. We also had raised vegetable and flowerbeds constructed and had the greenhouse re-glazed.

25   My Life in Dinedor in the 1950s

by Joyce Nicholls

My mum lived in Newcastle on Tyne before she came to Hereford, where she worked as a cook for the army. It was in Hereford that she met my dad, who was a farmworker in Dinedor.

My dad, Ken Nicholls, worked for Mr Jack Pugh who owned Upper Cross Farm; he was also in the Home Guard. Dad and mum got married at Much Birch Church, as at that time they lived at Wrigglebrook in Much Birch. Then, together with my older brothers Bobby and Stanley, they moved to Fairview Bungalow on Dinedor Hill to stay with Lottie and Arthur Isles who were brother and sister. Dad was later given a house on Lower Gatehouse Farm which had a large orchard and a big garden – my mum had returned to Newcastle in 1948 for my birth as it was a difficult pregnancy and on return extra space was needed. Then in 1950 my younger brother Ken Jnr was born.

Dinedor was a lovely place to live even though we had no electricity, television or any mod cons – very rural! You had to go down a field to get to our house so we could always tell if anyone was coming to visit us.

As kids we always had jobs to do. We had to go to Mr and Mrs Davies at the Raven Farm just off the Wonder Pitch to collect the milk every evening. The boys had to chop morning wood for the fire every day, and as I got older I used to go to the smallholding, The Gatehouse, next to ours, where Mr and Mrs Jim Davies and Des lived. On a Tuesday after

Our house at
Lower Gatehouse Farm

With Mrs Davies' calves;
Dinedor Hill is in the background

school, or in the holidays, I used to help pick flowers so they could take them to the Cattle Market to sell on a Wednesday.

Mr and Mrs Davies were always good to me. They used to take me to St Andrew's Church in Dinedor on a Sunday, and also on Sunday evenings when school holidays were on. I am sure that I am still a member of St Andrew's Church because I started so young!

There were always plenty of things to do, what with having my brothers to play with, and their friends coming over. Many a time we would go up Dinedor Hill and mum would say, 'Be back before dark!' We called everyone Mr or Mrs or Uncle or Auntie, and we would always be visiting someone.

On hot summer days we would take some bread and jam sandwiches up to the hill, and drink Mrs Holmes' homemade lemonade at the Tea Gardens. We always had a cooked evening meal.

In Mrs Davies' orchard

We always made a day of Dinedor Sports, attempting the races. It was all great fun!

As Dinedor School had closed we used to catch the school bus at the crossroads at the bottom of Dinedor Hill along with many other children including the Birch Boys, the Davies family, Kenny Powell and Derek Jones. The bus was always full, with some dropped off at Hunderton School and others at Whitecross School, Redhill Secondary Modern, Bluecoat and the High School.

We had no running water; it had to be carried from a few fields away. Sunday was bath night, when the tin bath would be placed in front of the fire. I was always first to have a bath as I was the girl, then the boys followed after me. I remember my dad building a well in the garden with his friend Stan Weavin;

Feeding one of Mrs Davies' calves

there were probably other people involved but he was the only one I can remember.

On bonfire night my dad always made a big bonfire. All the local kids would join us; dad would collect all the fireworks from them and then, after making sure all the animals were inside, we had a brilliant bonfire and firework display.

At Christmas dad would kill the geese and chickens, the boys would help feather them and I would help mum dress them so we could take them to the railway station, to be sent to Newcastle for mum's relations for their Christmas dinners.

When I was 11 we moved to Rotherwas as again we needed a larger house. Mr Pugh had sold the farm to Mr H.P. Goodwin, who had several other farms, so we got a bigger house. This time we had electricity, running water and a flush toilet; we were in heaven. We still lived in Dinedor and could still catch the school bus.

For several years in the summer holidays I had a job of showing people around Rotherwas Chapel and I would get the key from the Ministry Police Office at the top of our road.

I have to say my days in Dinedor were happy days, although hard work for everyone!

26 Garden Cottage, Dinedor

by Norma Forrest

The first memory I have is of sitting alone on a low, circular stone wall in the dappled shade of an ancient walnut tree, its dangling branches adorned with green fruit and translucent green leaves hiding me from the world. The tree and I lived at Garden Cottage, Dinedor, Hereford. It is the garden and the countryside surrounding it that hold most of the memories of my life spent living there, from 1 November 1945, when I was 18 months old, until 2 June 1950, when I was 6.

We were living in Dinedor because my father had got a job at the Hollow Farm, as herdsman to a large Friesian herd. Originally he had gone to work at the farm as a tractor driver, but on arriving he found out that that job was already taken, so he had no option but to take the vacant herdsman's job, for the going agricultural rate. He worked a full day from Monday to Saturday, and also every Sunday from 6.45 to 11.30 and then from 3.30 to 7.30 to do the milking, so he was unable to go to church and we could only go for family walks in the summer evenings. But why should he complain? After all, he was paid an extra pound for this Sunday work. So he bit his lip and said nothing. My father enjoyed working for Mr Gilander, though he was always aware that there was a line to be drawn between him and his boss, happily as they might work together, and Gilander had a reputation for a fiery temper.

I used to wander up the road hoping to see my dad working around the farmyard seeing to the cows and calves. There were several enormous Friesian bulls with brass rings in their noses tethered on the other side of the road in large metal-fenced pens. They had wild eyes and used to bellow away and paw at the ground. Once, one of them went mad with rage, tossed the metal gate up into the air and, out of control, ran across the road into the yard. My father then had the dangerous job of capturing him and taking him back to his pen. He was always worried about these unpredictable bulls (they were used for AI, Artificial Insemination) breaking free and harming his family. So I was never encouraged to hang around the farm or the buildings, let alone the fields where the bulls were kept.

My mother earned extra money by working in the dairy processing the milk into the churns for the morning collection by Cadburys. But one of the main factors in our household economy in those days was that Garden Cottage was a 'tied' cottage – that is, it was tied to the farm and there was no rent to pay. By verbal agreement, we could have as many potatoes, cabbages and pints of milk from the farm as we wanted. As a child I often heard my parents mention the words 'tied cottage'. These two words would bring my playing to a halt, and I would want to hear what they were about to say. Even at a young age, I wondered whether we were going to be the next family turned out on the side of the road in the rain and cold. I had heard so many stories when we travelled around to friends and relations, and of course there was always the local gossip that passed around from village to village, of people being evicted. I knew it was one of my parents' greatest fears, and I am sure that the fear of homelessness took a toll on the happiness of our family life.

Garden Cottage, and Mr and Mrs Gaines's cottage next door, were situated in and at the edge of a large old orchard, surrounded by a high hedged bank. On the other side of this bank the ground fell away into a deep ditch about eight to ten feet wide. Through our hedge, by way of a little metal gate, I had access to this meadow and then on to the church with its graveyard full of wild flowers. I took the same route to go to school every day. I remember little of the house except that it seemed pretty to me and had red-brick walls which were covered with a climbing vine that was green in summer and brilliant red in autumn before it dropped its leaves to the ground.

I was just 2 years and 8 days old when my beautiful baby sister Sheila Daryl took her first breath and broke the silence of the house, so I suppose I can't really remember it. But it is my wish to imagine her arriving into this world on a warm May day in 1946. I know that from my first glimpse I loved her, and we became like shadows of one another.

My family; I'm on the left

Inside the house there was a kitchen with an enormous Belfast sink in which my mother used to bath me every night. The house also must have had electricity, as I remember my mother ironing our cotton summer dresses with a sleek chromium-plated electric iron.

Joined to the house by a passageway was a reasonably sized outhouse. In the springtime this is where my father used to put the tiddling lambs from the farm to rear by hand. In the beginning there were only a couple, and my sister and I were overjoyed to give them their pop bottle full of made-up powdered milk. They were always ravenously hungry, and the milk would trickle out from both sides of their mouths, down onto their chests and onto the floor. Once the bottle was empty, they would try and suck our fingers. They became our pets. But within a week or two everything changed. By then there were a dozen lambs or more, making the most incredible din all the time. The lovely clean golden straw had become a sodden mess as streaming diarrhoea ran continuously from their backsides. With my hands to my mouth I ran outside and was almost sick with the awful stench. I would do no more lamb feeding, no matter how much the lambs called out, or how much my father wished me to. All this time my father battled away, continually scrubbing down and laying out new straw, but to no avail. The diarrhoea kept running. In those days there were no anti-biotics to stop the 'scours' so those poor little lambs suffered a lot. But my sympathies were with my father, who looked after them, trying to make their life as comfortable as possible. Thus, at an early age I learned not to be deceived by the popular image of fluffy white baby lambs. To me they were smelly, worm-infested creatures, best left to those who knew how to look after them.

It was in the pretty setting of Garden Cottage that I was to see four summers of our garden path edges turning a brilliant sky-blue with grape hyacinths, whilst in the middle plots healthy-looking vegetables grew all year long. Through all the seasons I spent my time rambling around our large orchard and the meadows beyond, which were filled with moss-covered fruit trees. But my favourite place of all was at the foot of the walnut tree with my small albino cat, 'Snowy', on my lap. Her coat was soft and warm to touch, and I would spend hours stroking her fur from the top of her head to the tip of her black-tipped tail.

We also had a grey long-haired Old-English-cross mongrel dog called Timmy. He was all long and lanky and great fun to be with, and he would follow us everywhere. But one day he ran out into the usually traffic-free road and straight in front of the coal lorry that was delivering the winter fuel. I can remember a lot of commotion outside on the road and the odd yelp coming from Timmy. Our parents were terribly upset, but managed to keep us all inside the house, and we never saw a thing. The next day we buried him in the orchard under an apple tree.

When I became tired of my garden and pets I would seek out Sylvia Wilcox and we would wander the fields on the lower slopes of Dinedor Hill. In spring, one tall hazel hedgerow at the side of a bridleway leading up to the hillfort had swathes of single pink primroses and sweet dark purple violets at its feet, and we would take home bunches for our mothers to put in tiny glass vases. I remember my father excitedly talking about a rare sighting of a red squirrel up there. But by the time I was old enough to keep still and quiet enough to hide from their view they had disappeared from Herefordshire altogether.

We would sometimes meet up with Clive Gilander and the little Cleland boy, whose dad had the big farm, and the little Baker boy who used to live with his family in one half of the vicarage. We used to roam through the orcharded, sleepy village, which comprised only a few houses, a church and the village school. There was rarely any motorised transport, which was a good job as we had no road sense. We were five mischievous children on the look out for anything interesting to play at.

One day we heard a great clucking from one of Mr Johnny Cleland's barns and realised it was a hen who had just laid an egg. We were frequently asked to go and find stray hens' nests, so into the barn we crept on hands and knees through an extra large rat hole in the bottom of the huge door. The great beamed barn was fully stocked with sweet-smelling summer hay, and we climbed through the bales looking for the nest. Eventually it was found and there, nestled in a warm hollow, was not just one but about a dozen brown speckled eggs. Normally it would never cross our mind to take any, but this time, there being so many, we decided each to take a few home for tea. As you can guess, I was told off in no uncertain terms for stealing the farmer's eggs, and my parents made me put my share back where I found them.

In high summer, when the sun scorched our skin a golden brown, my sister and I would seek out the shade of the house and, with some old battered baking trays and spoons given to us by our mother, would while away the hours making mud pies. We would decorate the tops with wild flower petals or marigolds and ferns if there were plenty, and then bake them in the hot sun until they were brick hard. The next day we would wet the top again and redecorate them with new petals and different patterns. Oh, to be a child again in the 1950s with such simple pleasures in life!

On Sunday afternoons, dressed up in my Sunday best clothes, I would walk to meet Sylvia Wilcox outside her house, and we'd cross the road together and go into the church for Sunday School. I suppose I must have enjoyed those afternoons because I have no memories of them being unpleasant but I have no idea what we did or what was said to us. Perhaps one can send a child too early for such teachings if the brain has not developed enough to remember them. We had kind and caring neighbours at Garden Cottage, and two of them, Mrs Wilcox and pretty Kathleen Gaines, became my godparents when I was christened with my sister, both of us wearing white dresses, in Saint Andrew's Church just across the orchard. My mother told me that I walked to my christening and that the service was part of the afternoon's Sunday School.

Like many others in the area, my parents were always on the look-out for ways to earn some extra money. One of the easier ways was to sell the surplus fruit from one's orchard. With the whole family at hand it was an easy enough job and in no time at all the bags of fruit would be stacked outside the gate waiting for the lorry to take it into Hereford and beyond. Sid Wright's in Hereford used to send a man around the country areas in the spring to persuade cottagers to sign a contract allowing Wright's to take all their fruit at an agreed price. This kind of agreement usually suited both cottager and wholesaler very well, but I remember that one year we and every other family had such a glut of damsons on our trees that the branches almost broke under the weight. Sid Wright's immediately went into action, knowing that they could not cope with such vast quantities of fruit. An employee arrived to count the bags that we had stacked at the gate and then gave my mother a chit for how much they owed her. She was then told to throw the fruit away. My mother and father, who could not stand to see good food go to waste, looked for someone to take all this fruit for free and, on seeing an advert in a local paper, sent it by freight train to an orphanage in west Wales. Whether it got to its destination is uncertain, as no letter ever arrived to say that it had been received.

We also took in lodgers. One of them, Hans Streitmater, was a German prisoner of war and had been sent to the Tupsley camp. I remember him as a tall man with dark hair and a gentle-looking face. He was ordered by the Ministry to come and work at the Hollow Farm. My mother was told by Mr Gilander that she must give Hans lodgings, and that she would be paid for this service. The trouble was that she had no bed for a lodger and no means of buying one. My grandmother came to her rescue and bought a single iron bedstead and mattress from Cresswells of Kington. It arrived within a week on the train from Kington to Holme Lacy Station. When we left Dinedor it was to become my brother's bed and eventually it ended its days filling a 'glat' in the hedge that surrounded our garden.

Our other lodger was John Dennis from Llanigon near Hay-on-Wye. He came to work at the Hollow on the same scheme as Hans, as there was a shortage of men to work on the land. My mother was kept very busy cooking and washing for three grown men, as well as us three small children. But she still found time to work in the dairy every day, chilling the milk from the Friesian herd and then cleaning all the equipment.

I have lovely memories of Hans and John. They were always gentle and kind, like big brothers I suppose, and would talk to us and push me for ages on the swing which hung from a branch of an apple tree. Hans particularly loved living with us, and he became a part of our family. After a day's work on the farm he would willingly help my mother with all the household chores. He was gentle and thoughtful, and whilst my mother caught up with some extra jobs he would read me and my brother bedtime stories. His mother was Polish and his father German, so he had no alternative but to go to war as part of the Hitler Youth, but he told my mother that he was glad when he was captured by the British as only then could he see the end of all the killing. He had seen one of his family taken away to a concentration camp. My mother and father kept in contact with him for years after we left Dinedor, and heard that eventually he had gained British citizenship.

I regularly used to wander down to Dinedor Cross as there were lots of families who lived in galvanised huts in a meadow near there, and lots of children could be seen playing around the place. I was the sort of child who always enjoyed my own company but I must have sought these children's friendship or else I would not have gone there so much. One pretty little girl was the same height as me, dark-haired as well, but she only had one eye. The other one was closed and the lid misshapen. I used to look at her through the gate and smile at her for I liked her, and she, with her thin little pale face, would smile back at me, her sole eye questioning my reason for watching her so often. Why did I not say 'Hello' to her? Why did she not say, 'Come and play with us'? The silence seemed so strange. I used to hear that they were 'refugees from another country' and could not speak any English. But I too was having speech difficulties and was a little girl locked away in a world of my own. I'd love to meet her today and say 'Hello,' and then the memory of two lonely little girls wanting to play together would be wiped away.

One year at Dinedor Church fete my Uncle Stan won the pig in the bowling competition and he gave it to my Dad to fatten up. But the keeping of pigs did not interest me at that time, and it just grew uglier and fatter by the day. Come autumn, the slaughterman arrived from Rotherwas but I don't remember anything about that.

On warm sunny days I remember having to walk all the way to Hinton, a matter of 3½ miles, where Mr and Mrs Blanche had their General Stores and close by was also a Post Office. Once there quite often we would walk into Hereford to buy other goods we needed. My fit and enthusiastic mother thought nothing of these little jaunts. Whilst I plodded along at her side, my baby sister was pushed along in style in the high pram. I remember putting on an act about having sore feet and aching legs, and quite often my mother took pity on me and I was sat in the bottom end of the pram and told to keep quiet. But when the cold weather arrived it was unthinkable to walk all that way. We would walk as far as Dinedor Cross, leave the pram in a shed

My father and Dobbin

which belonged to a friendly lady who lived close by, and walk the few hundred yards to catch the service bus to Hinton and then on into town.

When the River Wye broke its banks it would flood all the streets around the Old Bridge, which of course cut off Hereford city from the south. My brother and I found this really exciting. In fact it was probably the only time when he would come willingly to do some shopping with us. For the kind young soldiers from nearby Bradbury Lines would be lined up with their 'water ducks', (DUKW), waiting to give everyone a lift from one side of the flood to the other. In those days no-one complained about the blocked road. In fact it would not have been right for a winter to have passed by without the Wye bursting its banks and everyone being able to have the thrill of a ride in a 'water duck'.

As it happened, though, we were destined not to spend many winters living at Garden Cottage. The sacking of men working on the land was common at that time, and of course led not only to loss of livelihood, but to the eviction of the family from their home. In 1948 the Agricultural Wages Scheme was set up by the Labour government, and on the advice of his father, Harry Morris, but to the annoyance of Mr Gilander, my father, along with John Dennis, joined the Agricultural Union based at Holme Lacy for sixpence a week. From that day on, Gilander took a dislike to my father and one day, not in a good frame of mind, he ordered my dad to muck out the yard. This was not the first time that Dad had been asked to do something which was not in his area, but for the general farm worker to do. More importantly, my father had no time to do it, as all his working hours were spent looking after the very large milking herd. Probably feeling a little 'ognal' himself, Dad said that he was not going to do it. And with that, Gilander, who was not known for his patience, said, 'You do it Percy, or go down the road.' And that was that. My father collected his bait bag and walked down the road. He had been given the sack.

A couple of days later, Gilander asked my dad to leave the garden tidy and with all the vegetables growing in it for the next workman. He was willing to pay £20 for all this produce and fruit bushes. My father accepted the amount and signed a piece of paper, which he had not read, to say he had received the money. As you can guess, it was much needed. The following Monday, when my father went to the dole office, he was refused any money as they had been told over the phone that there was a job at the farm and that he had refused to do it. Also, he had signed a form to say that he had received all his dues. My father explained that he was the herdsman at the Hollow Farm, not the farm labourer, and had never refused the work that he had been employed to do. But they were not really interested, and he walked away empty-handed. The agricultural union was willing to take up his case and fight on his behalf so that he could be restored to his job. But my father said that he had had enough of the tied cottage system and was going to look for other employment.

Seven weeks were to pass before my mother had any real money coming into the house. In later years she told me that some days she did not know where our next meal was coming from. Save for her own mother sending her a five shilling postal order every week, which she could ill afford to do, and Mrs Edge, at the grocer's in Weobley, near to what would be our new home, letting her have groceries to be paid for when Dad's first pay packet came in, we would have starved. Although I was only 6 years old when we moved, I remember seeing my father looking very worried and my mother crying as she carefully packed up our few belongings and wrapped up her electric iron in a towel and put it away in our oak blanket chest. She knew that her days of having the luxury of a house with running water and electricity were over. We were to move to a much simpler house, with a spring for our water supply and paraffin lamps and candles for light. It was not until 1959 that I saw my mother unwrap her precious iron again.

On the morning of Tuesday 2 June 1950 our family moved from Garden Cottage (for the next day another herdsman and his family were to move in and take our place), and in the afternoon we moved into Ivy House, a two-bedroom black and white cottage near Weobley. Mr Jack Davies, a kind and understanding farmer, had offered my father a job and cottage right from the beginning, as Dad had truthfully explained our predicament. Gilander refused to give him a reference, but luckily he had kept the wonderful references that he had been given by previous employers and which had got him the job at the Hollow Farm in the first place. He was to be paid the agricultural rate, with the added bonus of as much wood as we wanted from Garnstone Hill, with permission of the estate. He was overjoyed, and to crown it all, by renting the cottage for five shillings a week, he had managed to beat the tied cottage system.

This move changed everything for our family and all for the better, at least in the short term. Jack Davies had a friendly housekeeper called Mrs Caudle, and in wet weather she allowed Dad to take his bait indoors by the hearth. He was also told that when any beasts were to be killed on the farm he would be welcome to take some joints back home. We thrived on our newly found freedom, and I remember my parents talking about the future and what they wanted from it, which was so different to the feeling of impending doom at Dinedor.

(This chapter is taken from A *Child of the Hedgerows,*
growing up in Herefordshire in the 1950s by Norma Forrest
and published by Logaston Press in 2013)

27   Life at Glebe Farm

by Vall Cleland

As a close neighbour to the church and Rectory, the school and School House, Glebe Farm has had its place firmly fixed in the centre of the community for several hundred years. As the

Mary Cleland looking after the sheep below the church wall.

Jane and Mary Cleland with Jolly, the last working horse on the farm.

Stan Weavin (farmworker) with Jolly and root cart, together with Jane and Mary Cleland.

John Thomas with Jane and Mary Cleland and a stack of sugar beet. John farmed the 28-acre Mill Farm where he kept shorthorn cows from which they made their own butter, but he also helped out at the Glebe. He was well known for his hedge-trimming skills.

name suggests it was originally owned by the Church, who rented it out to provide income. In 1914 the Cleland family became the tenants and shortly afterwards became owners of the farm. The Cleland family have farmed the property ever since.

28   Camp Dairy

by John Davies

Camp Dairy, run by my father Harry Davies, operated from the house that's now called Camp Cottage. The dairy probably began its life sometime before the start of the Second World War by supplying milk from a few cows kept on the smallholding's 17 acres. After the war, milk was purchased daily from Sellacks in St Owen's Street in Hereford, from where it

Harry Owen was my mother's younger brother, who lived at The Nest, further down the hill. He served in the army during the Second World War and won several cups for boxing, as shown in the photograph. He came out of the army a trained vehicle mechanic, and was very useful to my father in keeping his delivery van on the road.

Pam Davies with the van used by Harry Davies to deliver milk

*Jean Davies, Harry Owen, Mrs Davies and
Anne Davies haymaking at Camp Dairy*

was collected in 10 gallon churns. It was then delivered direct to customers from the churns, using pint measuring jugs. Later, the milk was bottled at the dairy and delivered to customers the following day. The daily delivery run gradually increased beyond the initial core of local people to private homes in many parts of Hereford and some pubs including The Lamb (now The Barrels) along with Bulmers Cider Factory (then based in what is now the Cider Museum).

29   Watery Lane Farm from the 19th to the 21st centuries

by Nicola Goodwin

The 1871 census is the first to mention Watery Lane Farm by its present name; before then there are details of many farms in Lower Bullingham but no exact reference to the site on Watery Lane. In that year 67-year-old William Magness was the head of the household, and farmed with his son William T. Magness who was 33. They had four servants living with them: Mary Jinkins aged 52, who was born in Madley, 12-year-old Jane Spires, who had been born in Worcester, 53-year-old Charles Powell, born in Hentland and 16-year-old George Powell from Dinedor.

By 1881 James Godsell (also spelled as Godsall) was the head of the house. He was 33 and a 'farmer of 110 acres employing 3 men and 2 boys'. He was born at Wormsley in Herefordshire and lived with his wife Emma, also aged 33, their daughter Marie who was aged 2 and two servants: Annis Davies aged 19 and 18-year-old Charles Powell, who lived in Dinedor. The census shows that there were six cottages at Moorlands, a hundred metres further up Watery Lane, which James Godsell leased in addition to the farm. He in turn rented them out and of the men living there one was employed as a gun maker, another as an engine driver and a third as a shepherd.

James Godsell farmed at Watery Lane for at least 30 years as he was still there in the census of 1911. By that time he was 64 and married to his second wife Sarah-Jane, aged 56. They had been married in 1895 and local legend has always surrounded what happened to the first Mrs Godsell, Emma, who is listed on both the 1881 and 1891 census. The story is that Emma had been walking in the fields and orchards with her daughter and they had got their skirts and shoes very wet. On return to Watery Lane Farm she was attempting to dry out in front of the fire when her skirt caught alight and she later died of her injuries. No record of her death has been found, so what actually happened to Emma remains a mystery.

James Godsell was the tenant of the farm when it was put up for sale alongside the rest of the Rotherwas House Estate on 5th September 1912. We can only imagine what it must have been like for James, who had been living and farming the land for more than three decades. Alongside Watery Lane Farm, the sale details show that he was renting two cottages at The Moorlands and an additional five acres of pasture and orchard land. His annual rent was £274.15 for Watery Lane Farm plus £20.50 for the cottages and extra land. We have no way of knowing if he bid for the farm at the sale which was held at the Green

Dragon Hotel in Broad Street in Hereford, but it was sold to a Mr Watkins from Luntley Court near Pembridge. The records don't show when James Godsell's tenancy at Watery Lane Farm ended, but he died in late 1915 aged 68. By the 1930s Watery Lane Farm was available for rent and Harold and Martha Goodwin took up the tenancy from the Watkins sisters, spinsters and the daughters of Mr Watkins who had purchased the houses and land in 1912.

In the early part of the 20th century, cider was sold from the mill on the side of the house and people used to stop by to buy a drink on their way to the tea rooms at the top of Dinedor Hill. The Rotherwas House Estate sale records show that in 1912 the tea rooms, then run by Mrs Elizabeth Wildman, were put up for sale alongside the cottage next door. They continued to be run as tea rooms after the sale and for many decades it was a popular walk for families and young couples who would come from the city and up Watery Lane

Watery Lane Farm in 1960

170

Aerial view of Watery Lane Farm in 1966. This shows the large number of buildings in the Rickyard parallel to the Holme Lacy Road, of which just two are still standing. The orchard and fields behind the farm now comprise The Shires and The Pastures housing estate.

to have tea in the café at the top of the hill and enjoy the views. Bert Daniels lived until he was 99 and said he had fond memories of the cider hatch on the side of the mill as the boys could get something to drink even if they were only 12 or 13. His grandfather was the gamekeeper on the Rotherwas Estate and lived at Keeper's Cottage on the top of the ridge between Dinedor Hill and Sink Green Farm, where the remains of a building can still be seen close to the triangulation pillar.

Harold and Martha Goodwin moved to Watery Lane Farm in the late 1930s, moving to Herefordshire from Powys where they'd been farming for six years. Martha was a member of the Layton family who have a long history of farming in Herefordshire but when they first rented the farm Harold's relatives thought that he was mad to consider farming so close to the city. At that time there were only a couple of dozen dwellings between the farm and St Martin's Church on the edge of the city and the largest building was the Poor Clare's Convent. The nuns made altar bread and used to give the remains to the farm for the cattle to eat.

In the 1940s, '50s and '60s there would have been at least a dozen men working on the farm full time – Harold and his three sons Harold jnr, Ken and Ralph, plus eight farmhands

– as well as lots of casual workers who were brought in to help with the harvest or the hoeing. They also sold milk and cream from the door of the house. The Goodwin family have continued farming at Watery Lane and in the surrounding area ever since, although livestock and dairy have made way for arable and orchards in the last few years.

Tracey Goodwin lived at Watery Lane Farm with his parents and grandparents and then moved back there with his family in the 1990s:

> We used to drive down the straight mile and have to go through sets of railway gates which were manned by MOD police. There was also lots of railway track left; the lines were kept well into the 1960s for dismantling trains and wagons and as a little boy that was a great place. It was really exciting to be able to jump up there and play with your friends.
>
> We used to graze sheep and cattle on the northern section and the eastern section. They used to open the doors of the old air raid shelters and wander in but then the doors would shut on them so we lost a few sheep which became trapped and starved to death. It was a fabulous place to play. There were rows of baths and sinks at one time but most of what remained was taken either legally or illegally.
>
> Garden Cottage on the old Rotherwas House estate was amazing during the 1950s and 1960s. It was rented by a gentleman who grew roses and other flowers for market gardens and it was like walking into a seed catalogue, it was so beautiful. In more recent times I went down to see the Smith family who were our tenants then. Their young boys were sitting on the sofa watching television and next to them was a small

Washing the sheep in the Red Brook before shearing in the early 1960s

pony, with its back end resting on the sofa next to them. You had to see it to believe it!

It saddens me that certain aspects of the area have disappeared. In the 1960s Rotherwas Park was stunning, full of big cedar trees and wild daffodils. At the time it was seen as the right thing to do and my grandfather had the trees removed, but it really saddens me as that would be such an asset to have on the edge of the city if it hadn't been destroyed. I'm pleased that the Enterprise Zone is now bringing jobs and money to the area and that some of the history is being preserved but the area has changed so much in the past century.

Watery Lane has been susceptible to flooding for at least a century, maybe more. The Red Brook now runs parallel to the road but the archaeological evidence shows that it originally went behind the site of the White House and down into the river close to Sink Green Farm. Whether it was re-routed naturally or for economic reasons is not known. Patricia Goodwin moved to the farm with her husband Harold in the 1950s, and her son Tracey has lived there both as a boy and then with his family in the 1990s:

TG - The worst flood that I can remember was in 1961. It lasted for seven or eight days and there was four foot of water in the lower rooms and two foot in the rest of the house. It came over the mantelpiece in the dining room.

PG - All we could see was the top bar of the gates on Watery Lane, the water was so high that it came rushing over the wall outside the kitchen.

TG - We had ladders so that we could get up to the first floor. Normally the water would come up and go down within two to three days but this lasted for more than a week. Some of the neighbours had a boat but we never did. We had a Fordson Major tractor and you stood up as there were no seats so you could still drive through the floods.

PG - It was business as normal for the farm. The cattle stood in the water and we milked them like that. They walked up through the water from the fields and then back down again, they didn't seem to mind.

TG - Floods were quite exciting in one sense but you quickly got bored with them because of how you had to live. We didn't ever have sewage come in then, just silt. The floors were stone and there is a well under the house so we were able to hose most of the house down.

When we renovated the house in the 1990s we had to take down most of the walls in the kitchen and pantry. We found big sheets of flat asbestos and plastic fertiliser bags behind that on batons. They'd thought that they were protecting the bricks but it just caused them to rot and they were just like powder. In some places the erosion was almost through the walls which were 20 inches thick. Because the walls dried out quickly they thought they were doing the right thing. My grandmother, Martha, also had the painters come in almost every year to re-paint the kitchen, larder and breakfast room so it always looked tidy – but behind the paint the walls were rotting.

The next worst flood in my memory was in October 1998 when it went through the whole floor. We heard the water gushing through the well which is under the breakfast room and then the water was coming up through the wooden floor in the dining room two steps up from that. We lifted up the carpet and it was coming up through the boards.

Since 2008 the River Wye has been fantastic and has been going up and down much more quickly. The flow of water is going down to Chepstow far quicker than it used to. In January 2014 the water was within an inch of going in the house but luckily it didn't go inside.

30   A Miscellany

Charities
Pye's Charity. The sum of 8s-6d, received yearly by this parish, from Pye's Charity has not been distributed for 4 years. The last distribution was made in 1832, when £1-5s-6d, for three yearly payments, was given among poor householders who were not receiving parish relief.

We recommended that the sum of £1-14s, now in the hands of the churchwarden in respect of the charity, should be distributed immediately among the most deserving poor of the parish who were not in the receipt of weekly pay, and that, on account of the smallness of the sum, the future distributions should be made every alternate year.

Canon's Dole. The 30 loaves received every Christmas and Candlemas from the Canon Bakehouse at Hereford are distributed by the churchwarden immediately after their receipt, among all the most deserving poor belonging to the parish, in equal shares, each person receiving one loaf.

Herefordshire Charities 1836

Hereford Mechanics Institution Rural Excursion
The members and their friends intend to take tea together upon Dinedor Camp on Whit Monday, May 31st 1841 at 6.0 o'clock in the evening. A Promenade Band will be in attendance from 4.0 o'clock and perform during the evening. The presence of ladies will afford the highest gratification to the Committee and members. Members tickets including tea and refreshments, 1d each, non-subscribers 2d, to be had of the secretaries. Each member is privileged to introduce a friend at the first named price.

N.B. No tickets will be issued after 6.0 o'clock on Saturday night.

Hereford Journal, *May 1841*

Holy Wells
It was formerly the custom in Herefordshire farmhouses for the servants to sit up to see the New Year in, and at midnight to rush for the 'cream o' the well', the first water drawn from the well in the year, which was thought to be beautifying and lucky. The maid who succeeded in getting it would take it to the bedroom of her mistress, who would give a present for it. 'My missus always had the cream o' the well to wash in on New Year's morning,' said Mrs M ---,

'and she always put a shilling under the basin for me, too.' Duncumb (in 1804) says of one at Dinedor: - 'a well in this parish excites much emulation on New Year's Day in a contest for the first pailful of water, which is termed "the cream of the well", and is presented to some neighbour as a mark of respect, and a pledge of good fortune; a pecuniary compliment is expected in return.'

The Folklore of Herefordshire
by Ella Mary Leather, 1912

Dinedor Hill

Brooklands, Hay, Hereford,
November 11th, 1912

Dear Hutchinson,
You remember our pleasant little jaunt to Hereford and 'Oyster' Hill, (*sic* Dinedor Hill), where the Romans were supposed to eat oysters!!! And where there was such a beautiful view. Well, in an old book the other day I found out the reason of its being called 'Oyster' Hill, which, of course, means the Hill of Ostorius. It is as follows: – 'The first Roman General who penetrated into South Wales was Ostorius Scapula; he established several garrisons in that country, which were afterwards attacked

John & Susan Jones of Rose Cottage, Dinedor Hill. John was a wheelwright and coffin maker. He died in 1894.

and overpowered by the natives; vexation produced by this circumstance is supposed to have hastened his death, – Cum taedio, Lxii 39, curarum fessus Ostorius concessit vita – (Taciti Annales L12 0.3) to which I must refer you if you wish any further information. No doubt he established his garrisons in Wales from his hill near Hereford, kind regards, yours sincerely, E. Cambridge Phillips.

Woolhope Club Transactions, *1912*

Heronry

Miss Cowley of Hereford had drawn the Club's attention to the fact that the heronry at Rotherwas had been destroyed and that the birds had started a new breeding place at Dinedor Hill, but this was in danger of extinction, the trees in which the birds had nested being marked for felling. The trees at Dinedor belonged to the City of Hereford Corporation, so the Hon. Secretary approached that body with the request that those appropriated by the herons might be spared. The Corporation had acceded, a matter upon which they as a Naturalists' Club might congratulate themselves (applause). This was probably the only heronry in England on public property.

Woolhope Club Transactions, *1918*

Top: Mrs Shuker on horseback outside Dinedor Court circa 1917.
Her daughter, Doris Jones, stands in the background on the left
Bottom: Doris Jones on horseback outside Dinedor Court, with Mrs Shuker standing in
front of the horse. Doris worked in the munitions factory and played in their football team,
though she was a Land Army girl at one stage of the war.

Flood
At Putson and Bullingham there are three small wooden bridges carried on stone masonry piers, spanning the mouths of three small streams which enter the river here. One of these was at the Clare Sisters Convent. There was formerly a stone and brick bridge of one arch here, but a cloudburst on Dinedor Hill in July 1851, caused such a rush down Watery Lane that it was washed away.

Woolhope Club Transactions, 1922

Stone Age Axe
Mr Coulson, aided by the scratching of his little dog, unearthed a very fine polished green stone axe from the flat, level space just within the north-east corner of Dinedor Camp.

Woolhope Club Transactions, 1923

Water Supply
The parish is dependent on wells and springs, but locally supplies are inadequate. The well at Mr Southall's bungalow alongside the railway at Sink Green is 60ft deep in Old Red marl and sandstone, and yields a satisfactory supply.

Wells and Springs of Herefordshire, H.M.S.O., 1935

Dinedor village coach party to Barry Island, 1936.
The majority of those shown lived on 'the hill'.
In the front row, from left to right: Cynthia Yapp (young girl), Amy Maddox holding Tracy
Yapp; Kathleen Holmes; Ms Grismond; Melvyn Holmes (with football) and Mrs Gosling.
In the back row: Two unknown ladies and young child, Elsie Lamb (in white dress),
Susan Yapp, Emmey Birch (in dark coat), Annie Andrews, Charlotte Isles, Audrey Weavin,
Mrs Nash, Harvey Jones, the coach driver (centre with tie), Blanche Matty, Louise Holmes,
unknown lady, Doris Holmes, Billy Gosling, Reg Jenkins, James Holmes,
Mrs Gilbert and Mr Gilbert

To celebrate the Coronation of 1953, villagers wore fancy dress and after attending a special church service several football matches were held. This picture shows the married ladies' team, who played a match against the single ladies.
Front row kneeling, left to right: Margaret Thomas, Winnie Price, Ann Evans and Mrs Halliwell
Back row: Betsy Jones, Katie Holmes, Cynthia Yapp, Marion Lamb, Dot Thomas, Zilla Davies, Peggy Davies and Joyce Lamb.
The litte girl on the right is thought to be Jane Cleland

References

Chapter 1   Introduction

An overall source was: Hunter, J and Ralston, I. (eds), *The Archaeology of Britain: An Introduction from Earliest Times to the Twenty-First Century*, Second Edition, (Routledge, 2009)

1. British Geological Survey, *1:50 000 Series, England and Wales Sheet 215, Ross-on-Wye, Solid and Drift Geology*, (Natural Environment Research Council, 2000)
2. Nash-Williams, V.E., *The Roman Frontier in Wales*, (Board of Celtic Studies of the University of Wales, 1952)
3. Garmonsway, G.N. (ed.), *The Anglo Saxon Chronicle; The Abingdon Chronicles, C,* (J.M. Dent & Sons Ltd, 1953)
4. Wilson, John Marius, *Imperial Gazetteer of England and Wales* (1870-72)

Chapter 2   The Prehistory of Dinedor & Rotherwas

1. Interview on BBC Hereford & Worcester with Nicola Goodwin
2. John and Margaret West, *A History of Herefordshire*, 1985, p.20

Chapter 3   Landscape Change in Dinedor

1. Arnold, C.J and Davis, J.L, *Roman & Early Medieval Wales*, Sutton Publishing Limited (2000), p.36-37
2. Rees, Revd W.J., M.A. F.SA (ed), *The Liber Landavensis, Llyfr Teilo: with an English translation and explanatory notes*, The Welsh MSS Society (1840)
3. *ibid*
4. Garmonsway, G.N. (ed), *The Anglo Saxon Chronicle; The Abingdon Chronicles, C.* J.M. Dent & Sons Ltd (1953)
5. Yorke, B., *The Kings and Kingdoms of Early Anglo-Saxon England*, Routledge (1997), p.125
6. Wood, M., *The Story of England*, Penguin Books Ltd (2010), p.101
7. Coplestone-Crow, B., *Herefordshire Place-Names*, British Archaeological Reports (B.A.R.), British Series 214, (1989)
8. Rees, *op.cit.*
9. Hamerow, H., *Early Medieval Settlements: The Archaeology of Rural Communites in Northwest Europe 400-900*, Oxford University Press (1992)
10. Wood, p.105)
11. Thorn, Frank and Caroline (ed). *Domesday Book, Herefordshire*, Phillimore (1983), 8,7
12. Thorn, 25,1
13. Fenwick, C., (ed) *The Poll Taxes of 1377, 1379 and 1381: Part 1: Bedfordshire – Lincolnshire*, The British Academy (1998), p.xiv
14. ibid, p.180-1)
15. Atkinson, C., *Site of Medieval Village, Dinedor: An Archaeological Field Survey*, Herefordshire Archaeology Report Number 327 (2013)

16. Rátkai, S., *Dinedor DV13: The Pottery: An archaeological pottery report*, Birmingham (2014)
17. Rackham, O., *Trees & Woodland in the British Landscape: The complete history of Britain's trees, woods and hedgerows*, Phoenix Press (2004, Fourth Edition), p.147
18. Copplestone-Crow
19. Taylor, C., *Fields in the English Landscape: Archaeology in the Field Series*, J.M. Dent & Sons Ltd (1975), p.71
20. Rátkai
21. Atkinson, C., in prep
22. Webb, J., (ed) *A Roll of the Household Expenses of Richard de Swinfield, Bishop of Hereford, during part of the years 1289 and 1290*, The Camden Society (1853), p.220
23. Stone, D., *Decision Making in Medieval Agriculture*, Oxford University Press (2005), p.45-6
24. Wood, p.188
25. Herefordshire County Records Office IR29/14 57-74 APP4
26. Rackham, p.152-4
27. Taylor, p.75-7
28. Harnden, J., (ed). *The Hearth Tax Assessment for Michaelmas 1665 for Herefordshire and comparison with the Herefordshire Militia Assessments of 1663*, (1984)
29. *ibid*
30. *ibid*
31. Kain, R.J.P, Chapman, J. and Oliver R., *The Enclosure Maps of England and Wales, 1595-1918: A Cartographic Analysis and Electronic Catalogue*, Cambridge University Press (2004)
32. Census data obtained from: A *Vision of Britain through Time* (www.visionofbritain. org/uk/unit/10035727/cube/TOT_POP), date accessed: 16th April 2014

Chapter 4   Rotherwas House
1. Coplestone-Crow, B., *Herefordshire Place-Names*, British Archaeological Reports (B.A.R.), British Series 214, (1989)
2. Thorn, Frank and Caroline (ed). *Domesday Book, Herefordshire*, Phillimore (1983)

Chapter 6   St Andrew's Church, Dinedor
1. Jakeman and Carver, *Directory and Gazetteer of Herefordshire*, (1890), p.193
2. Vincent, N. http://www.historytoday.com/archive/history-today/2002/volume-52-issue-6 accessed 25th February 2014
3. Dinedor with Holme Lacy PCC Mini Guide, *Welcome to St Andrew's Dyndor*, (1988), p.2
4. Brooks, A. and Pevsner, N., *The Buildings of England: Herefordshire*, (Yale University Press, 2012) pp.198-199
5. pers.comm. B. Ferris 2014
6. *Welcome to St Andrew's*, p.2
7. *ibid*
8. Davison, C., *The Hereford Earthquake 1896*, (Cornish Bothers, 1899), p.19

9. *The Buildings of England: Herefordshire*
10. *ibid*
11. e.g. John 1:36; Revelation 5:12,13; 14:1; 21:22
12. Revelation 1:8
13. pers.comm. S.J. Savage 2014
14. *Welcome to St Andrew's*, p.4
15. Marshall, G., *Fonts in Herefordshire part 2*, (The Woolhope Naturalists' Field Club, 1950), p.40
16. pers.comm. B. & E. Edwards 2014
17. *Welcome to St Andrew's*, p.5
18. pers.comm. B. & E. Edwards 2014
19. PCC minutes for Dinedor with Holme Lacy, 9th April 1987
20. The possible reasons underlying the association between the yew tree and churchyards are fascinatingly discussed by R. Mabey in *Flora Britannica*, (Sinclair-Stevenson, 1996), pp.28-37.
21. *Flora Britannica*, p.421.
22. pers.comm. B. Ferris 2014
23. *The Buildings of England: Herefordshire*
24. pers.comm. B. Ferris 2014
25. The team member was responsible for Ballingham and Bolstone for at least some of this time, pers.comm. A. Stoakes 2014
26. *Diocese of Hereford Institutions 1539-1900*, (Wilson and Phillips, 1923), p.170
27. This is the content of a document displayed near the font in the space under the tower in the church
28. Swinfield (trans. and ed. W.W. Capes), Hereford Diocesan Register vol 2 1283-1317, (Wilson and Phillips), p.125
29. *Diocese of Hereford Institutions*, p.53
30. *ibid*, p.131
31. *ibid*, p.170
32. A photocopy is said to be held in the stores of the South Wye Team office, but could not be found
33. *Welcome to St Andrew's*, p.3
34. Muckleston Family History Group, http://www.mucklestonfhg.com/Pages/MainPage40.aspx accessed 21st February 2014
35. *ibid*, http://www.mucklestonfhg.com/Pages/TheywentintotheChurch.aspx
36. *Church Calendar and Clergy List for the Diocese of Hereford 1948*, (Orphan's Printing Press, 1948), p.76
37. Russell, J., http://www.herefordtimes.com/archive/2001/07/26/5701384. *Pews for thought as front room hosts Sunday worship*
38. pers.comm. B. Ferris, S.J. Savage and R. Gorman 2014
39. pers.comm. S.J. Savage 2014
40. PCC minutes for Dinedor with Holme Lacy, 3rd May 1990

Chapter 8   Trade and the River Wye at Dinedor

1. Survey 1697, HRO AP21
2. Barge Accounts, Landscape Origins of the Wye Valley Project (LOWV)
3. H. Hurley, *Herefordshire's River Trade*, Logaston Press (2013)
4. Barge Accounts, LOWV
5. J. Price, *City of Hereford*, p.193; Towing path survey GRO Q-RU M 14
6. Rotherwas, Dinedor Heritage Group 2009; Barge accounts, LOWV; *Hereford Journal* 28 Nov 1810
7. G. Farr, *Chepstow Ships*, 1954; Barge accounts LOWV; Bullingham tithe map 1844
8. Tupsley documents G87/57/8; Tupsley tithe map 1839
9. G. Lipscomb, *Journey into South Wales*, 1802, p.76; Shoesmith & Eisel, *The Pubs of Hereford City*, 2004, p.312

Chapter 9   Rights of Way, Roads and Railways

1. Geoffrey N. Wright, *Turnpike Roads*, Shire Publications, 1992; Heather Hurley, *Trackways to Turnpike, The Old Roads of South Herefordshire*, 1992
2. William H. Smith, *Herefordshire Railways*, Sutton Publishing, 1998

Chapter 10   A hundred years of Dinedor occupations, 1851-1951

The following Directories and sources have been consulted: Post Office Directory of 1879 and 1856; Kelly's Directories of 1885, 1891, 1895, 1900, 1905, 1909, 1913, 1917, 1929, 1934, 1937 and 1941; Kent Services Directory of 1950/51, an unidentified Directory of 1851; Cassey & Co Directory of 1858; Bailey's Directory of 1858; Littlebury's Directory of 1876/7; Jakeman & Carver's Directories of 1890; 1902; 1914; Sale Catalogue of Rotherwas Estate 1912

Chapter 11   Dinedor Men in the Great War

The following sources were consulted: Commonwealth War Graves Commission; Medal Index Cards WO373 – ancestry.co.uk; Silver War Badge Roll WO329 – ancestry. co.uk; Soldiers Service Papers WO363 – ancestry.co.uk; Sailors Service Papers ADM/188/784 – National Archives – Kew London; Pension Papers – ancestry.co.uk; Prisoner of War records – National Archives – Kew London; *Herefordshire in the Great War* by William Collins ; *Hereford Times* 1914–1919 – Hereford Record Office; Herefordshire Absent Voters List 1918 – Hereford Record Office; 1911 Census for Herefordshire – ancestry.co.uk; Sunset Militaria Dinedor Cross – Military Archives; John Davies, son of Harry Davies.

Chapter 13   The Dinedor Secret Army Patrol, 1940-44

The following sources were consulted: *The Mercian Maquis* by Bernard Lowry & Mick Wilkes, Logaston Press, 2002; *Auxiliary Units History & Achievements 1940-44* by Maj N.V. Oxenden MC, October 1944; *Operation Sealion* by Richard Cox, Anchor Press, 1975; *Some Talk of Private Armies* by Len Whittaker, Albanium Publishing, 1984; Auxiliary Patrols Nominal Roll WO199/3389 – National Archives Kew London; *Hereford Times* 6 February 2014

Chapter 17   Quarries and Stone Buildings

1. htt.herefordshire.gov.uk
2. www.bgs.ac.uk/mineralsUK/buildingStones/StraetgicStoneStudy/EH_project.html

Index of Names

General Index

Also from Logaston Press

Walking the old ways of Herefordshire
History in the landscape explored through 52 circular walks

by Andy & Karen Johnson

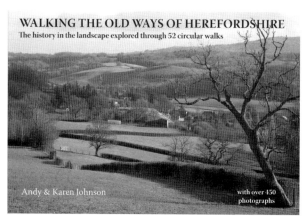

The walks in this book have been chosen with the aim of exploring Herefordshire's past, with each walk passing or visiting a number of features about which some background information is given. These include churches, castle sites, deserted medieval villages, landscaping activity, quarrying, battle sites, dovecotes, hillforts, Iron Age farmsteads, Saxon dykes and ditches, individual farms and buildings, squatter settlements, almshouses, sculpture, burial sites, canals, disused railway lines – to name but a few, and including some that can only be reached on foot.

They have also been chosen to help you explore Herefordshire's present, to breathe its good air, from south to north, west to east, from quiet river valleys to airy hilltops, from ancient woodland to meadows and fields, from remote moorland to the historic streets of the county's towns, and of course Hereford itself.

The walks range from 2½ to 9½ miles in length, with the majority being between 3½ and 6½ miles. Each walk has a sketch map and detailed directions, together with background information about features en route.

The combination of photographs and historical information, together with the index, make this more than simply a book of walks, but also a companion to and celebration of Herefordshire.

Paperback, 384 pages, over 450 colour photographs and 50 maps.   Price: £12.95

Also from Logaston Press

Herefordshire's River Trade
Craft & Cargo on the Wye & Lugg

by Heather Hurley

The story of the trade on the rivers Wye and Lugg in Herefordshire has never been told in its entirety – until now. Local historian Heather Hurley has delved into barge accounts, the pages of the *Hereford Times* and *Hereford Journal*, and the papers of firms and businesses based on or near the banks of the two rivers to produce this account.

It covers the type of craft used, the cargoes carried, the families of boat owners, the masters and crew of the boats, accidents on the water, the development of wharves, the hiring of bowhauliers and the advent of the horse towing path. Perhaps most surprising is the extent of boat building along the banks of the Herefordshire Wye, with craft ranging from small ferries to barges and even steam-powered vessels.

But the story is wider than just the rivers and their banks, for it is also about the felling and transporting of timber to supply the shipyards at Plymouth and elsewhere building vessels for the Royal Navy, the need to reduce the price of coal in Hereford, the trade in cider, wine and spirits, and the requirement of lime for agricultural and building purposes. There are also hints of the lifestyles of some of those living near the Wye, indicated by the goods that were ordered and transported by boat.

Paperback, 208 pages, 190 illustrations over half in colour.   Price: £12.95

Also from Logaston Press

The Mercian Maquis: The Secret Resistance Organisation in Herefordshire and Worcestershire during World War II

by Bernard Lowry and Mick Wilks

Formed in 1940, at the same time as the Home Guard, its members were recruited from amongst a tightly-knit farming community and from those in other reserved occupations. Organised into patrols of about half a dozen men and knowing their locality intimately, their role would have been to carry out acts of sabotage and terror behind the German invader's lines whilst the Regular Army regrouped for counter offensives. The establishment, operation and function of the 12 patrols formed in Herefordshire and Worcestershire are fully explained, together with information on the even more shadowy world of the Special Duties spies and urban saboteurs. From carefully camouflaged underground Operational Bases liberally supplied with explosives and arms and constructed in woodland on high ground, patrol members would have set out at night to harry the invader. This was to be done in the knowledge that they and their families risked summary execution if captured.

Paperback, 160 pages, 70 black and white photos and plans.   Price £10

Roses round the door?
Rural images, realities & responses: Herefordshire, 1830s-1930s

by Tim Ward

Tim Ward's collection of postcards, built up over many years, includes many images of Herefordshire's past rural life: harvesting and hop-picking, cidermaking and cattle breeding, blacksmiths, beekeepers and basketmakers. Behind these carefully posed photographs were the working lives of men and women – lives that were far from a 'roses round the door' country idyll. This book is made up of a combination of those images and an attempt to tell the story behind the pictures. Sometimes dispossessed by the Enclosure Acts that took common land from rural people and forced them into miserable working and living conditions, Herefordshire's agricultural labourers, like those in other parts of Britain, eventually found a voice, with the formation, from 1871, of a succession of farmworkers' unions.

Tim Ward charts the history of the unions, the strong characters who founded them, including Thomas Strange, William Gibson Ward, Joseph Arch and Sidney Box, and what became of their attempts to bring about change for those whose cause they championed. The story unfolds against a backdrop of a fast-changing world, including a number of factors that would change rural life for ever – mechanization, opportunities to leave the land and find a new life in the industrialized cities, or even abroad, and the onset of the First World War.

Paperback, 168 pages with 135 black and white illustrations.   Price £12.95